Dedication

I would like to dedicate this book to my best friend and brother, Thomas Earl Gaines who has been privileged to rest in the presence of God since May 19, 2009!

Table of Contents

CHAPTER 1 .... Zion, Get Ready for Judgment
CHAPTER 2 ....Money Hunger Leaders
CHAPTER 3 .... United We Stand, Divided We Fall
CHAPTER 4 .... Names and Nature of God
CHAPTER 5 .... Yeshua Ha'Mashiach or Jesus Christ
CHAPTER 6 .... The Greatest Sacrifice
CHAPTER 7 .... Secrets behind Closed Doors
CHAPTER 8 .... Strongholds of Depression
CHAPTER 9 .... Silence of Abuse
CHAPTER 10 .... RED ALERT: Cycle of Abuse
CHAPTER 11 .... Mended but Broken
CHAPTER 12 .... ENEMY IN ME-Self Destruction
CHAPTER 13 .... Power of the Holy Ghost
CHAPTER 14 .... My Brother, My Friend
CHAPTER 15 .... Wrestling with our First Love
CHAPTER 16 .... Power and Control in Religion
CHAPTER 17............................ Step Out of Religion

Introduction

      With all the religions of the world, no one can truly find peace within himself. We all know that God is not the author of confusion, nor does He uphold to division. God dwells in the heart of man and He is eternal, there is no beginning or end to Him. I believe that Satan planted religion in the heart of man, that we may forsake the will of God and follow our own will; as he did in heaven.

      Religion doesn't allow you to freely worship God nor will you truly love others. Without a true relationship with God, Satan's chains bind us tight around the post of religion, which ultimately leads to sin against God. But a true and honest relationship with God breaks the chains of tradition and religion: alongside doubt, heartache, pain, poverty, and condemnation. Only as we worship, our spirits have been "released from captivity to soar in the presence of God!" "Our answer lies not within man or nature, but in the Lord!" Surrendering means "letting go of your desires" I don't understand why we accept religion instead of a relationship with God.

      The life of the heart is a great place of mystery, yet we have many expressions to help us express this flame of the human soul. In the end, it doesn't matter how well we have performed, or what we have accomplished- a life without heart, is meaningless. For out of this wellspring of our souls flow all meaningful work, all real worship, and sacrifice.

      There is a secret place set within each of our hearts. It often goes unnoticed, we can barely put words to it, but yet it guides us throughout the days of our lives. You may not always be aware of your search, and there are times you have abandoned looking altogether, but again and again, it returns to us; this yearning that cries out for the life we all desire, Life in Relationship to God.

1

Zion, Get Ready for Judgment

<u>1Peter 4:17</u>
The time has come that judgment must begin at the house of God;
and if first begin with us; What shall the end be of them that obey
not the Gospel of God?

The message of physical prosperity has become more popular for us to hear; therefore our desire to spread the gospel has become secondary. In recent years, as the Holy Bible says; many have turned away from sound doctrine and chose to listen to fables and follow pastors who say things tickling of their ears." Who don't want to hear about money, money, money in such a time as now? Our economy is getting tough and many are losing their freedom due to outrageous debt, and there seems to be no way around such turmoil and heartache.

Nearly every home in America and global are affected. Within the last decade, there has been a great rise of pastors who has embraced the message of prosperity, and we have followed their ways and found out that many are only wolves in sheep clothing, making millions of dollars and raising crazy offering to benefit themselves and not the body of Christ as a whole.

I've been to several mega churches, wherefore the pastor's sermons are centered on prosperity and many have taught that salvation means "more things for you," and if you don't obtain such things you are living beyond your means as a child of God or in error with God. Many in the congregations belittle themselves and try to live up to those materialistic expectations. But when they do not receive the so-called finer-things in life, many lose hope in God, run back into sin, and reject His love. I must take the time to remind you; Jesus says that we can only have one master, yet because we live in a materialistic world, and Satan knows what we like, and the times we are living in, the deception behind physical prosperity is overlooked by many.

We travel across town to hear the next "feel-good "message, and literally jump out of our clothes when we hear messages pertaining to receiving a new home, car, or substantial amount of money in the bank. But when judgment hits the house of God, we murmur and complain, curse our leaders, and leave the ministry.

Again, I don't want to say that physical prosperity is bad, because God does desire for all of His children to prosper naturally, but I will ask; "What good is it to teach believers about storing up physical things, when many are lacking in the area of soul prosperity? God desires for us to prosper both physically and spiritually and we must understand there are prinicipals we must live by in order to maintain the blessing we receive.

Jesus asked in His word, what does it profit a man to gain the world and lose his soul? What can man give in exchange for his soul? As long as our mind is focused on the things of this world, the devil can cause us to lose our focus on God and slowly drift away into sin, usually through money.

Our desire for money and the finer things of life may be innocent, but if we focus our attention on our wants not being met, and become competitive against others with tangible things, our relationship with God becomes second-hand. Can you honesty say that God, and not money, is your master? One test is to ask which one occupies more of your thoughts, time, and efforts.

We should never get fascinated with our possessions, lest they possess us. Please don't forget, the Lord promises to supply our needs according to His riches and glory. Whatever you store up, you will spend most of your time and energy thinking about. I encourage all please don't fall into the materialistic trap, because "the love of money is a root of all kinds of evil."

Our divine purpose is to be a light unto this world; which walks in darkness. The light is nothing other than love. Many of us, feel very comfortable inside the church building, but somehow, allow fear keep us from walking the streets. Please don't be confused: God does not dwell in building made of stone, but in the heart of man.

Our purpose in life is not to attend church every Sunday, but rather to go out from the church building to the streets, "strategically" enriching the souls of the lost with the message of salvation through Christ Jesus and His Holy Word. Have we not noticed young kids are being killed daily, strung out on drugs, raped, incarcerated, and ruled by the strongholds of homosexuality, bisexuality, drugs, witchcraft, pornography, and suicide, while we huddle in a building like we are at a sporting event and entertain one another with feel-good messages?

It is sad to admit this but I must be truthful, for quite a while I felt and believed television ministry was good enough and there is no need for us to go out into the streets.

I even had the audacity to say foolish things like; "we are to separate ourselves from sinners and be holy!" Again I would like to say for several years, I have been taught through doctrines of man (religion), that followers of Jesus are to keep away from sinners, but one night the Lord rebuked me openly; "Myron who are you to think you are all-that, you are only saved by My grace and I called you to be a witness of Me by spreading My Word and walking in Love!" And to add a token to the rebuke from the Lord, He simply asked me…"Did I shed my blood and die for your sins only?" Did I not command you to go out into the world and make disciples in My Name?"

Truthfully, we as a people need to be more effective witnesses to the lost and we also need to walk in love with a pure heart. If we have a heart to serve the Lord and walk in His will, the world that we live in will be more receptive to the call of Salvation. Yet because we hold to traditions and philosophies of the church, we blindly take hold to the mind-set of the Pharisee's (religious folks) whom lived amongst Jesus.

Don't ever forget, Jesus showed us all by example what God commands us to do in life. When the Pharisee saw Him sitting amongst sinners and tax collectors (crooked people) they replied to his disciples (as in a form of mockery), what is "your Master" doing sitting with sinners and scam-artist?" and they probably added (as in a form of mockery); "Isn't He (Jesus) called the Holy-One? Why is He relaxing with unholy people?" (Matthew 9:10-13) My dear brothers and sisters, as long as we continue to huddle in church buildings afraid of the world and the prince of the world (Satan), evil will continue to have victory and we be cast into the lake of fire for not fulfilling God will; SOUL HARVEST for the kingdom of God!

The Lord was driven with compassion towards the sick, lame, and spiritually dead and followed the commandments of the Father. He would literally be grieved in His heart to see one in low-positions or lost. How many of us can truly say we have the same heart of Christ within?

Many of us have seen and know the Passion of Christ, now I ask you do you have passion for Christ and are you willing to die for Jesus and lose everything for His name? Are we as the body of Christ willing to minister the uncompromising Word of God, without taking into consideration our life?

I must agree my dear brothers and sisters, the harvest is truly plenteous, but the laborers are few. (Matthew 9:36-38) I tell you the truth, if we truly knew and appreciate the extent of pain, humility, and sacrifice Christ went through to redeem our souls back to God; we would be driven with compassion and joy to spread the good news to the lost. I tell you the truth, we do not deserve the grace of God, we do not deserve the mercy of God, and we surly do not deserve the love of God. My dear brothers and sisters, its time to make a change; remember God has given us power against all the works of Satan and we have the key of life, which is the teachings of Jesus Christ, His prophetic life and the mighty power of His blood, to unlock the door of those who are imprisoned in their mind.

As long as Satan can get us away from the importance of the cross and the gospel of the Kingdom of Heaven and caught up in the material prosperity messages, he can cause us to receive lies and not fulfill our purpose in life. The demons that roam the earth are not playing games; they work 24 hours a day, 7 days a week, destroying the souls of Gods children while we play church and "prophe-lye"! We need to stop playing church and be the church God has ordained us to be!

2

Money Hunger Leaders

<u>Matthew 6:24</u>
No man can serve two masters; for he will love one and hate the other; or he will hold to the one, and despise the other; ye can not serve God and mammon.

Our economy is getting tough and many are losing their freedom due to outrageous debt, and there seems to be no way around such turmoil and heartache. Nearly every home in America and global are affected. Again, as stated in Chapter 1, within the last decade there has been a great rise of pastors who has embraced the message of prosperity, and many have followed their ways and found out that many were only wolves in sheep clothing, making millions of dollars and raising crazy offering to benefit themselves and not the body of Christ as a whole.

Foolishly, yet knowingly, we follow them and later find out that we have been deceived by the devil through them. Many may preach a good message, dress in the finest clothing, and may have the holiest walk (posture), but fake as a counterfeit dollar. So fake, that he tries to buy the ability to look more holy or godly in front of people.

I have been affiliated with several church organizations wherefore the leaders may push and prime their members to give out more tithe and offering, by saying things like…"Now church, we have a budget that has to be met within this month, we are short $1000; which is okay. But when they use slogans like…"the Lord has shown me that some of you are holding back; I know there is a couple of you that can give a hundred or two hundred dollars"; my spirit immediately gets vexed.

As a form of threat, knowingly or unknowingly, I heard some even say to the congregation, "Now church we will be here all night, we are not leaving until we come up with the money!" Many televised ministries use this slogan as a means to blossom: "in order for you to receive your blessing from God you must sow into our ministry such and such amount of money each month, and then your breakthrough shall come to pass."

Truthfully that is crazy, because many are not truly taught the ways of the Lord, they have been taught the ways of man. So instead of us seeking the Lord for guidance we blindly accept any feel good message from our leaders and find ourselves in more of a financial crunch than we were before. Now when I began to speak of the hidden dangers of the church and the wolves in sheep clothing, people have a tendency to dog me out or accuse me of coming against them or "touching God's anointed." The question that goes through my mind is simply; why?

I've come to a conclusion, for a long time I found myself in their position: I was in love with the image of the pastors, wanting to please the leaders, therefore I carelessly gave, gave, and gave until I landed in a world of debt and rebuked by God Almighty for such selfish deeds. I was not even taking in consideration of my soul being delivered from the bondage of Satan or the lost being added to the kingdom of heaven, all I wanted to do was get out of the rat-race of debt and land into my promise land of blessings.

I have been in church services where manipulation and control were so strongly manifested; it was very obvious by anyone with any sense of spiritual discernment. Here are some of the occurrences that I have observed:

1. Manipulating people into financial giving by quoting un-Biblical formulas - i.e. if you give a certain amount of money, you will receive a 100 - fold (highest possible) blessing.

2. Money lines - i.e. - people are placed into lines in front of the church based on the amount of money they gave ($25, $50, $100) and certain blessings are pronounced on these individuals with of course the highest monetary givers receiving the largest "blessing".

3. The sale of items to accomplish a particular need in your life - i.e. various colored cloths to place under pillows bringing about such things as mates for marriage, healing, and financial gain.

4. Forced words of a so-called prophetic nature whereby people are provoked to "prophesy" because a church leader will strongly imply God has something to say to his people. If no one speaks up, the people are made to feel guilty and unspiritual so someone will speak a word, obviously not from God because when God speaks, life-changing events occur.

Clearly Jesus name is being strongly manipulated and used as some type of magical chant that as long as we are claiming things by merely stating His name, it most assuredly will become ours and we most assuredly must receive whatever we ask. My observation of these occurrences did not just take place on a few occasions, but was considered a regular part of church services that occurred frequently.

I personal know people, who have been manipulated to give, give and give to the church and as a result of doing so; their finances and livelihood have been ruined. I could state additional examples but I wanted to share enough in hopes of your ability to share in my concern and grief over this plight. Many believe these incidences are a normal part of church services, and cannot and do not discern the elements of witchcraft that are involved. Many times in church services of this nature, the preacher appears more of a magician practicing and inducing magical occurrences than preaching the Word of God.

I pray that you understand, I am not opposed to claiming the promises of God of physical blessings He desires all His children to obtain; however, many times I have seen where people are provoked to claim things just for the asking that may not be within God's Will for their lives or in His timing or not at all ever meant to occur in their lives. I have also seen people take the Scriptures, "We can have what we say"..."Whatsoever we ask in Jesus Name He will do it"...etc. and claim personally motivated things for their lives that fill the lust of the flesh, lust of the eye, and pride of life. So the other Scriptures are taken and by verbalizing the Name of Jesus (i.e. I claim this house in Jesus Name) we use His name like He has to obey this type of request only because we asked for the thing in His name.

Many pastors urge their congregation to seek after these things, stirring up passions and lusts for things, without consideration of their relationship with God. In other words, why do we think we desire the blessing of God when we are not even walking after the Spirit or not seeking Gods way of doing things, or not presenting ourselves as Holy Sacrifices?

In these last and final days, we need to wake up and stop calling everyone that you see on TV or in front of a crowd a "man of God".

Check the scriptures for yourself and get closer to God and allow Him to open your eyes to the truth of His Word. Trust what the unction of Holy Ghost is trying to tell you and I believe you will not be fooled if you examine everyone with the words of God. And once you begin to do that, you will begin to see that you are bewitched by a spiritual scam and whom you thought, was a sheep was a wolf after your money! The power of the Holy Ghost is not only in us to keep us from falling into sin or being victorious over the works of Satan, but so you can spot the wolves/snakes in the pulpit. You can tell when your leader cares for your soul, or when they want your money.

We are in a day when there are more wolves on TV, or in the pulpit now than sheep. When your money is targeted and you become victimized by the very people that look like men and women of God; I encourage you to pray to God that He may raise your level of anointing within, so you can discern who is for Him and who is for themselves.

3

United We Stand, Divided We Fall!

1 Corinthians 12:25
There should be no division in the body, But the members should care for one another.

After careful research, I was able to conclude that there are more than 300 denominations in the United States churches alone and according to the World Christian Encyclopedia (year 2000 version), globally Christianity had 33,820 denominations with 3,445,000 congregations, and churches composed of 1,888 million affiliated Christians.

God built one church and that all saved people were in that church. He prayed for unity and rebuked division. Denominations as we know them did not exist till centuries later and only birth forth division. If we really want to please God, we must forsake what we want and practice what He wants because our whole duty is to fear God and keep His commands. We should be determined to do God's will, not our own.

To follow Jesus one must deny self. True religion does not consist of what pleases us; it is entirely a question of, what pleases God? Do you truly believe God is please with denominations or does He want unity instead? The only way to know what God thinks is to study His revelation, the Bible. So, what does the Bible say about denominations. Ephesians 3:10, 11; says the church is part of God's eternal wisdom. This shows that the church is important to God, so we should respect His will regarding it.

The word "church" is used two ways in the Bible: The "universal" church refers to the body or group of all saved people everywhere. It includes all who have been redeemed by Jesus blood, have been forgiven of their sins, and have been born into His spiritual family. Bible examples of this usage are: Matthew 16:18 - Jesus promised to build His church. The church is built on Jesus and belongs to Him ("my church"). Ephesians 5:23, 25 - Jesus is Head of the church, and He is Savior of His body. The "universal" church consists of all saved people everywhere because, when God saves people, He puts them in the church. In this sense, the church is always singular.

The "local" church refers to a congregation of followers of Christ, in a region who have united to work and worship together. According to the Bible, they have a pattern of organization, work that they are to do, and funds they use to do this work. Note that, in this local sense, the word "church" can be used in the plural - "churches of Christ" (Rom. 16:16). Congregations existed in different localities, but they were not religiously divided. All had the same pattern of organization, doctrine, worship, salvation, etc.

Denominations are not in the Bible, so they must have come from men. If we participate in them, we are following man's wisdom, not God's. They constitute a change in God's plan and we can easily read the Holy Bible and see that this is so. Do you believe God is pleased with people who defend their denominational background? Everything religiously which God did not plant will be rooted up. By whose command do denominations exist? Who planted them? Not God, but man. Hence, anyone who worship and do service unto Go in vain will be rooted up.

Each denomination has practices that contradict and disagree with the practices of other denominations. One says only immersion is true baptism; another says sprinkling is acceptable too. One says a child of God can fall from grace; another says this is impossible, etc. Surely this constitutes religious division and confusion. Yet the denominational concept says God will accept all of this- people in all the groups please Him and will receive eternal life. "It doesn't matter what you believe as long as you worship God sincerely," etc.

Is this really what the Bible teaches? John 17:20-23 - Jesus prayed for all who believe on Him to be one as He and His Father are one. We claim that He is our head, yet we practice division! Someone may claim the denominations are all part of one universal church, though they contradict one another. But is this how Jesus and His Father were one?

True Biblical unity consists of everybody doing the will of the Father! 1 Corinthians 1:10-13 - Paul pled with the Corinthians that there are no divisions among them (verse 10). Do denominations obey this plea? Are there "no divisions among them?" Surely they are divided, so how can anyone excuse their existence and say God will accept them?

Is Christ divided (verse 13)? Does He contradict Himself or teach contradictory things to His followers? Surely not! Such actions would make Him a hypocrite! How then can all the denominations be truly following Him and truly accepting His headship when they contradict one another? It must be true that some people are really not following Him and that is why the division exists. If Paul rebuked the division at Corinth, should we not rebuke the far greater division in our churches? Did Paul tell the Corinthians to just overlook their differences because they were all pleasing to God anyway? Not at all! He told them to cease their divisive practices and seek unity by practicing the true teachings of God.

Ephesians 4:3-6 - We must keep the unity of the Spirit. This means that, for the seven things listed, there is only one of each in God's true plan. Specifically, there is one true God and Father. Likewise there is only one true body and only one true faith, and the body is Jesus' church (Ephesians 1:22, 23; 5:23-25; Col. 1:18, 24).

It is just as essential to believe in only one true body and only one true faith, as it is to believe in only one true God. Denominationalism takes the one true body and chops it up into many disagreeing bodies having different and contradictory faiths. If all the churches are following Jesus, yet they are going in opposite directions, doesn't that mean Jesus is leading people in opposite directions? When people try to justify denominations, they make Jesus ridiculous and hypocritical! I encourage you to refuse to be part of any group that claims to be a denomination, or which excuses, justifies, or condones denominationalism.

4

Names and Nature of God

Exodus3:13-14
And Moses said unto God, Behold, when I come unto the children of Israel, and shall say unto them, The God of your fathers hath sent me unto you; and they shall say to me, what is his name? What shall I say unto them? And God said unto Moses, I AM THAT I AM: And he said, Thus shalt thou say unto the children of Israel, I AM hath sent me unto you.

We must understand that the names of God used in the Holy Bible act as a roadmap for learning about the characteristics of God. Since the Bible is God's Word to us, the names He chooses in scripture are meant to reveal His true nature to us. I have done careful research and feel it is important for us to understand the names and nature of God for personal commune with Him and also to avoid conflict with others whom may use one of the below names we may not know, in our witness unto them.

"ELOHIM" (or *Elohay*) is the first name for God found in the Bible, and it's used throughout the Old Testament over 2,300 times. *Elohim* comes from the Hebrew root meaning "strength" or "power", and has the unusual characteristic of being plural in form. In Genesis 1:1, we read, "In the beginning *Elohim* created the heaven and the earth." Right from the start, this plural form for the name of God is used to describe the One God, a mystery that is uncovered throughout the rest of the Bible.

Throughout scripture, *Elohim* is combined with other words to describe certain characteristics of God. Some examples: *Elohay Kedem* - God of the Beginning: (Deuteronomy 33:27). *Elohay Mishpat* - God of Justice: (Isaiah 30:18). *Elohay Selichot* - God of Forgiveness: (Nehemiah 9:17). *Elohay Marom* - God of Heights: (Micah 6:6). *Elohay Mikarov* - God Who Is Near: (Jeremiah 23:23). *Elohay Mauzi* - God of My Strength: (Psalm 43:2). *Elohay Tehilati* - God of My Praise: (Psalm 109:1). *Elohay Yishi* - God of My Salvation: (Psalm 18:47, 25:5). *Elohim Kedoshim* - Holy God: (Leviticus 19:2, Joshua 24:19). *Elohim Chaiyim* - Living God: (Jeremiah 10:10). *Elohay Elohim* - God of Gods: (Deuteronomy 10:17).

"EL" is another name used for God in the Bible, showing up about 200 times in the Old Testament. *El* is the simple form arising from *Elohim*, and is often combined with other words for descriptive emphasis. Some examples: *El HaNe'eman* - The Faithful God: (Deuteronomy 7:9). *El HaGadol* - The Great God: (Deuteronomy 10:17). *El HaKadosh* - The Holy God: (Isaiah

5:16). *El Yisrael* - The God of Israel: (Psalm 68:35). *El Ha Shamayim* - The God of The Heavens: (Psalm 136:26). *El De'ot* - The God of Knowledge: (1 Samuel 2:3). *El Emet* - The God of Truth: (Psalm 31:6). *El Yeshuati* - The God of My Salvation: (Isaiah 12:2). *El Elyon* - The Most High God: (Genesis 14:18).

Immanu El - God Is With Us: (Isaiah 7:14). *El Olam* - The God of Eternity (Genesis 21:33) *El Echad* - The One God: (Malachi 2:10). "ELAH" is another name for God, used about 70 times in the Old Testament. Again, when combined with other words, we see different attributes of God. Some examples: *Elah Yerush'lem* - God of Jerusalem: (Ezra 7:19). *Elah Yisrael* - God of Israel: (Ezra 5:1). *Elah Sh'maya* - God of Heaven: (Ezra 7:23). *Elah Sh'maya V'Arah* - God of Heaven and Earth: (Ezra 5:11). "YHVH" is the Hebrew word that translates as "LORD".

Found more often in the Old Testament than any other name for God (approximately 7,000 times), the title is also referred to as the "Tetragrammaton," meaning the "The Four Letters". YHVH comes from the Hebrew verb "to be" and is the special name that God revealed to Moses at the burning bush. "And God said to Moses, 'I AM WHO I AM; and He said, thus you shall say to the sons of Israel, I AM has sent me to you... this is My eternal name, and this is how I am to be recalled for all generations'" (Exodus 3:14-15).

Therefore, YHVH declares God's absolute being - the source of everything, without beginning and without end. Although some pronounce YHVH as "Jehovah" or "Yahweh," scholars really don't know the proper pronunciation. The Jews stopped pronouncing this name by about 200 A.D., out of fear of breaking the commandment "You shall not take the name of YHVH your God in vain" (Exodus 20:7). (Today's rabbis typically use "Adonai" in place of YHVH.)

Here are some examples of YHVH used in scripture: YHVH *Elohim* - LORD God: (Genesis 2:4). YHVH *M'kadesh* - The LORD Who Makes Holy: (Ezekiel 37:28). *YHVH Yireh* - The LORD Who Sees/provides: (Genesis 22:14). YHVH *Nissi* - The LORD My Banner: (Exodus 17:15). YHVH *Shalom* - The LORD of Peace: (Judges 6:24). YHVH *Tzidkaynu* - The LORD Our Righteousness: (Jeremiah 33:16). YHVH *O'saynu* - The LORD our Maker: (Psalm 95:6). The LORD who revealed

Himself as YHVH in the Old Testament is revealed as Yeshua (Jesus) in the New Testament.

Jesus shares the same attributes as YHVH and clearly claims to be YHVH. In John 8:56-9, Jesus presents himself as the "I AM." When challenged by some Jewish leaders regarding His claim of seeing Abraham (who lived some 2000 years earlier), Jesus replied, "Truly, truly, I say to you, before Abraham was born, I AM." Those Jewish leaders understood that Jesus was claiming to be YHVH. This is clearly established when they tried to stone Him to death for what they considered blasphemy under Jewish Law.

It is very important that we understand the names and nature of God mainly to avoid conflict in our life with others. Secondly, when we pray for a specific thing or petition the names we use can enhance our commune with God the Father. The names and nature of God are plainly characteristics of Him. But I will conclude there is no name above the name of Jesus in either heaven or earth below. When we call on the name of Jesus the angels tremble in the heavens and the demons flee. For He is the only man who has destroyed all the works of the wicked one Satan and has all power, glory, dominion, and majesty, to the glory of God the Father! Amen!

5

Yeshua Ha'Mashiach or Jesus Christ

I believe it is most proper to call Him *Yeshua*. I found more comfort in saying "Yeshua" in my prayer language and commune with God. I began to study upon His name and pronounce it slowly "Ye-shu-a." Surprising to me I began to understand it in a broader sense and began to worship Him more earnestly. I would simply say "Jesus" throughout my life but change never truly took place in my life until I began to study the Hebrew name of Jesus and watched the Passion of the Christ. The name Yeshua sounds so romantic and meaningful therefore I embrace it with full assurance of knowing Him.

Just think of His name in proper context and meaning, as God said He is: Redeemer, Strong Tower, Almighty God, Healer, Great I AM, Root and Offspring of David, Son of God, etc. Start saying "Yeshua' and if we say it slowly in remembrance of what God said His name is, and the many characteristics of Himself, you will be able to break it down in three syllables: "Yes-U-Are." Yes, Yeshua is Savior, Lord, God, Anointed One of God, etc.

Again when I began to say Yeshua and understood the pronunciations, it is a full manifestation of His characteristics. As I continually grow in the ways of the Lord, His name becomes more meaningful and precious. There are many who just say Jesus and not fully understand the power of His name and still chose to live life as a defeated foe, but I choose not to because I understand and have come into a relationship with God through His Son (spirit, DNA, offspring, seed) Yeshua Ha'Mashiach. But whether you pronounce it Yeshua or Jesus, there is power in His name and I am not here to debate or say what is right or wrong for God is judge and for me to sit in His position would be foolish.

I believe the Son of God proper name was Yeshua, indeed. God appointed and chosen Him as "Savior of humanity" and commanded Mary to name Him "Yeshua." Only in Hebrew does this name have any meaning. In Hebrew Yeshua means both "Salvation" and the concatenated form of Yeshua is "Lord who is Salvation."

There are many Yeshua's that we may read about in Biblical text and many are confused with the Yeshua who would later become the "Christ". The name Yeshua appears 29 times in the Tanach. Yeshua (Joshua) of Nun is called Yeshua in Nechemyah (Nehemiah) 8:17. Yeshua is the name of the Cohain HaGadol (the high priest) in the time of Zerubavel in Ezra 3:2. It is the name of a Levite under King Hizkiyah (Hezekiah) in 2 Chronicles 31:15. There is even a city called Yeshua in the Negev of Yehudah in Nechemyah11:26. Yeshua is also a shortened version of the word Yeshua much like Bill is for William.

In Paul letter to the Colossians in chapter 4, verse 11, there is a Justus called Yeshua a fellow worker of Shaul. Josephus, the famous Jewish historian mentions 20 different Yeshuas' (Jesus'), 10 of which are contemporary with Yeshua HaMashiach. All together, at least 50 Yeshuas from his time plus about 9 in the Tanach have been revealed from Biblical text and other literary sources.

Yeshua is a Hebrew name, which has been transliterated into Greek as *Iesous* (IhsouV: pronounced "ee-ay-SUS"). The English "Jesus" comes from the Latin transliteration of the Greek name into the Latin *Iesus*. Now Greek has no "y" sound, but the Latin "i" is both an "i" and a "j" (i.e., it can have a consonantal force in front of other vowels), the latter of which is properly pronounced like the English "y" (which explains the German *Jesu*, "YAY-su") That is why we *spell* Jesus as we do, taking it straight from Latin, but we *pronounce* the name with a soft "j" sound because that is what we do in English with the consonantal "j".

The first letter in the name Yeshua ("Jesus") is the yod. Yod represents the "Y" sound in Hebrew. English speakers mispronounce many names in the Bible that begin with yod because the yod in these names was transliterated in English Bibles with the letter "J" rather than "Y". This came about because in early English the letter "J" was pronounced the way we pronounce "Y" today.

All proper names in the Old Testament were transliterated into English according to their Hebrew pronunciation via the Latin, but when English pronunciation shifted to what we know today, these transliterations were not altered. Thus, in Jerusalem, Jericho, and Jordan have known such Hebrew place names as ye-ru-sha-LA-yim, ye-ri-HO, and yar-DEN; and Hebrew personal names such as yo-NA, yi-SHAI, and ye-SHU-a have become known to us as Jonah, Jesse, and Jesus. To further complicate matters, there was no letter "J" in the old English alphabet and the letter "I" was often used in its place. Often in early texts of the time, Jesus or Jerusalem would be spelled Iesus or Ierusalem.

The second sound in Yeshua's name is called tse-RE, and is pronounced almost like the letter "e" in the word "net". Just as the "Y" sound of the first letter is mispronounced in today's English, so too the first vowel sounds in "Jesus". Before the Hebrew name "Yeshua" was transliterated into English, it was first transliterated into Greek. There was no difficulty in transliterating the tse-RE sound since the ancient Greek language had an equivalent letter, which represented this sound. And there was no real difficulty in transcribing this same first vowel into English.

The translators of the earliest versions of the English Bible transliterated the tse-RE in Yeshua with an "e". Unfortunately, later English speakers guessed wrongly that this "e" should be pronounced as in "me," and thus the first syllable of the English version of Yeshua came to be pronounced "Jee" instead of "Yeh". It is this pronunciation that produced such euphemistic profanities as "Gee" and "Geez".

Since Yeshua is spelled "Jeshua" and not "Jesus" in most English versions of the Old Testament (for example in Ezra 2:2 and 2 Chronicles 31:15), one easily gets the impression that the name is never mentioned in the Hebrew Scriptures. Yet 'Yeshua' appears there twenty-nine times, and is the name of at least five different persons and one village in the southern part of Yehudah ("Judah").

In contrast to the early biblical period, there were relatively few different names in use among the Jewish population of the Land of Israel at the time of the Second Temple. The name Yeshua was one of the most common male names in that period, tied with Eleazer for fifth place behind Simon, Joseph, Judah, and John. Nearly one out of ten person's known from the period was named Yeshua.

The first sound of the second syllable of Yeshua is the "sh" sound. The Hebrew letter shin represents it. However Greek, like many other languages, has no "sh" sound. Instead, the closest approximation, the Greek sigma, was used when transcribing "Yeshua" as "Iesus". Translators of English versions of the New Testament transliterated the Greek transcription of a Hebrew name, instead of returning to the original Hebrew. This was doubly unfortunate, first because the "sh" sound exists in English, and second because in English the "s" sound can shift to the "z" sound, which is what happened in the case of the pronunciation of "Jesus".

The fourth sound one hears in the name Yeshua is the "u" sound, as in the word "true". Like the first three sounds, this also has come to be mispronounced but in this case it is not the fault of the translators. They transcribed this sound accurately, but English is not a phonetic language and "u" can be pronounced in more than one way. At some point the "u" in "Jesus" came to be pronounced as in "cut," and so we say "Jee-zuhs."

The "a" sound, as in the word "father," is the fifth sound in Jesus' name. It is followed by a guttural produced by contracting the lower throat muscles and retracting the tongue root- an unfamiliar task for English speakers. In an exception to the rule, the vowel sound "a" associated with the last letter "ayin" (the guttural) is pronounced before it, not after. While there is no equivalent in English or any other Indo-European language, it is somewhat similar to the last sound in the name of the composer, "Bach." In this position it is almost inaudible to the western ear.

The Hebrew Language Academy, guardian of the purity of the language, has ruled that it should be sounded, and Israeli radio and television announcers are required to pronounce it correctly. There was no letter to represent them, and so these fifth and sixth sounds were dropped from the Greek transcription of "Yeshua" -the transcription from which the English "Jesus" is derived.

So where did the final "s" of "Jesus" come from? Masculine names in Greek ordinarily end with a consonant, usually with an "s" sound, and less frequently with an "n" or "r" sound. In the case of "Iesus," the Greeks added a sigma, the "s" sound, to close the word. The same is true for the names Nicodemus, Judas, Lazarus, and others. English speakers make one final change from the original pronunciation of Jesus' name. English places the accent on "Je," rather than on "sus." For this reason, the "u" has been shortened in its English pronunciation to "uh."

      Today's traditional pronunciation of His name as "Jesus" has indeed obscured His true name, "Yeshua," and has shifted its perceived meaning much like most of His original teachings. But the greatest change that will take place is revealed in the book of Revelations, wherefore God has said Yeshua will have a name that has not been known to mankind, written on His forehead and thigh when He returns in all glory, power, dominion, and majesty of the Father. To the glory of God the Father and His Son Yeshua Ha'Mashiach!

6

The Greatest Sacrifice

I realized that I had taken the crucifixion less for granted all these years--that I had grown callous to its horror by an easy familiarity with the grim details and formed a distant friendship with Him who gave **His** all for **my** sins. The infinite **spiritual** suffering of the Incarnate God in atonement for the sins of fallen men I have no competence to discuss. However, the **psychological** and **anatomical** aspects of our Lord's suffering we can explore in some detail. That is, what did the body of Jesus actually endure during those hours of torture?

Crucifixion is the execution of a person by **fixation** to a cross. The Persians apparently first knew it. Alexander and his generals brought it back to the Mediterranean world--to Egypt and Carthage. The Romans apparently learned the practice there and (as with most everything the Romans did) rapidly developed a high degree of efficiency and skill in carrying it out. The most common form used was the "T" or *Tau* cross, which was comprised only of two parts: the *stipes*, an upright pole or beam, and the *patibulum*, or cross arm piece. This was the common form used at the time of Christ. It was efficient, quick, and deadly. There is overwhelming evidence in recent archaeological findings that this was the most common type used.

The upright post (stipes) or beam was permanently fixed in the ground with a notch at the top into which the patibulum or crossbar could be slipped without trouble. This crossbar would weigh from one hundred to one hundred and twenty pounds and the condemned man was made to carry this to the site of execution. It was during the Dark Ages that the cross was depicted in paintings, giving us the impression that Christ carried the entire cross. These same painters also placed the nails in the hands, again a misconception, for they would easily strip out through the fingers. If we turn to the early scholars of both modern and ancient anatomy, we always find that the forearm is included in the anatomy of the hand. This does not refute the saying of Jesus to Thomas, "Behold My hands."

The initial agony and suffering began in the garden of Gethsemane when Christ knew His time had come. Luke tells us, "And being in agony, He prayed more earnestly: and His sweat was as it were great drops of blood falling down to the ground"

(Luke 22:44). Jesus was under extreme physical and mental anguish and His sweat glands became bloody. This intense and abnormal condition is known as *hematodrosis*. This process of bloody sweat started the weakening and possible shock of the physical body of our Savior. After the arrest in the middle of the night, Jesus had six trials--all containing **unjust and false** accusations.

When He was brought before the Sanhedrin and Caiaphas the high priest, He suffered the first physical trauma. They mocked Him, spat on Him and struck Him continually in the face without any remorse. In the morning, Jesus was taken to the Fortress Antonia (part of which remains today) where Pilate examined Him and passes the responsibility to Herod Antipas. At the hand of Herod, Jesus suffered physical mistreatment also and then was returned to Pilate. It was then that Pilate ordered Barabbas to be released and condemned Christ to scourging and crucifixion.

There is much disagreement among the authorities as to the scourging. This was Roman, not a Jewish, custom. The hands were tied high to a tree or post. A whip was made of a short wood handle and heavy leather straps bearing usually the sharp bones of sheep knuckles or lead balls on the ends. The Jews forbade more than forty lashes (thirty nine was the maximum allowed), but the Romans did not have this limit. A Roman soldier usually carried out the scourging. The whip was brought down upon the bare back, cutting the skin first; then as the beating progressed, the muscles were laid bare, bruised and bleeding with marked loss of blood.

In a significant number of instances this was enough to kill a man. Ribs were broken, nerves exposed. Both venous and arterial bleeding occurred. Large deep, dark, bruised surfaces began to appear. Finally the skin of the back is hanging in long shreds. The whole area is an unrecognizable mass of torn, bleeding tissue.

Again and again, Jesus was beat to a bloody pulp' and knocked unconscious. The Roman soldiers did not keep count of the many blows Jesus received because He was condemned for blasphemy and causing uproar in the towns, and under Roman jurisdiction. Now the half-fainting Jesus was untied and slumped to the pavement wet in His own blood. The Roman solders saw great jest in this provincial Jew claiming to be a king. They throw a robe across His bleeding shoulders and place a reed in His right hand and pressed a crown of thorns upon His head. The crown was made up of flexible branches covered with long thorns (commonly used as firewood).

Again there was copious bleeding because the scalp is one of the most vascular areas of the body. After mocking Him and striking Him across the head, driving the thorns deeper into the scalp, more blood was lost. Finally tiring of their sadistic sport, they tore the robe from His back causing large clots of blood and scrum to stick to the robe and His back wounds were opened up again to massive bleeding and excruciating pain, almost as if He were being whipped again.

In deference to Jewish custom, the Romans return His garments. The heavy patibulum was tied across His bleeding shoulders. As he attempted to walk straight, He fell constantly due to the scourging, and tremendous blood loss from the brutal beating from the Roman soldiers. While in disgust, pain, and shock, the centurion hammered a large spike in the wrist of one arm, then the other. The arms are not stretched taut but are left sagging to allow flexion and movement. The patibulum or crossbar is then attached to the top of the stipes. Quickly His feet are nailed, the left then the right, with the same size large crude nail. They are nailed through the arch of the foot leaving the knees in a flexed position. As another form of mockery the title "King of the Jews" was nailed to the top of the cross.

With the knees flexed toes downward, the full pressure of the body is placed on the nerves of the feet. When this can be tolerated no more, the body sags to where the entire body weight is borne by the nails through the forearm. This produces excruciating pain on the median and ulnar nerves of the hand until this can be tolerated no more. Again the knees are straightened as much as possible.

This process of seesawing up and down further weakens and exhausts the body. At this point, great waves of cramps sweep over the entire body, the arms fatigue, and then the legs fatigue. Hanging by His arms, the pectoral muscles are paralyzed and the intercostals muscles are unable to act. Air can be drawn into the lungs but cannot be exhaled. Jesus fought to raise Himself in order to get even one short breath. Finally, carbon dioxide builds up in the lungs and bloodstream and the cramps partially subside.

Spasmodically, he is able to push himself upward to exhale and bring in the life-giving oxygen. It is most likely that during this time He utters the seven short sentences, which are recorded. The first is uttered while looking down at the Roman soldiers throwing dice for his seamless garment: "Father, forgive them for they know not what they do." The second is to the penitent thief: "Today thou shall be with Me in Paradise." Then looking at the terrified and grief-stricken John, he said: "Behold, thy mother," and looking to Mary, His mother: "Woman, behold thy son." The fourth cry is from the beginning of Psalm 22: "My God, my God, why hast thou forsaken me?"

Jesus endured hours of limitless pain, cycles of twisting, joint-rending cramps, intermittent partial asphyxiation, searing pain as tissues are torn and stretched from the nail wounds. His lacerated back yields to unrelenting pain as He plies up and down on the cross of rough timber. Then another agony began a deep crushing pain deep in the chest as the pericardium (a sac around the heart) slowly fills with fluid due to the extreme trauma and shock. Psalm 22:14: "I am poured out like water and all my bones are out of joint; my heart is like wax; it is melted in the midst of my bowels."

It is now almost over. Loss of tissue fluid has reached a critical level; the compressed heart is struggling to pump heavy, thick, sluggish blood into the vital tissues. The tortured lungs are making a frantic effort to gasp in small gulps of air. The markedly dehydrated tissues send their stimuli to the brain-- Jesus gasps His fifth cry, "I thirst." Let us remember another verse from the prophets in Psalm 22:15; "My strength is dried up like a potsherd and my tongue cleaveth to my jaws and thou hast brought me into the dust of death."

A sponge soaked in posca, the cheap, sour vinegar wine that is the staple drink of the Roman legionnaire, is lifted up to His lips. He apparently doesn't take any of the liquid. The body of Jesus was in *extremis* and He could feel the chill of death creeping through His tissues. This realization brings out His sixth words, probably little more than a tortured whisper, **"It is finished."** His mission of atonement has been completed. Finally, He can allow His body to die. With one last surge of strength, He once again presses His torn feet against the nail and straightens His legs, takes a deeper breath and utters His seventh and last recorded cry: **"Father, into thy hands, I commit my spirit."**

In order not to profane the Sabbath, the Jews asked that the condemned man be removed from the cross. The Romans usually left the bodies on the cross to rot. The common method of ending a crucifixion was fracturing--the breaking of the bones of the legs--preventing the victim from raising himself to breathe. The victim then died from suffocation.

Remember God's most precious gift to man was **His Only Begotten Son.** His saving power is free **if** we but obey his commands. Do we understand just how deep and all encompassing this love is? I think not; if it were so, then all mankind would be brothers and **love** would abound everywhere. Solomon said, "The conclusion, when all has been heard is ... fear God and keep his commandments for this is the whole duty of man" (Ecclesiastes 12:13). Jesus whose crucifixion we have just reviewed, said: "Come to Me all who labor and are heavy laden and I will give you rest. Take My yoke upon you and learn from Me for I am gentle and lowly in heart and you will find rest for your souls. For My yoke is easy and My burden is light" (Matthew 11:28).

7

Secrets Behind Closed Doors

Ecclesiastes 12:13-14
Let us hear the conclusion of the whole matter: Fear God and keep His commandments, for God will bring every work into judgment, including every secret thing, whether good or evil.

What are secrets? Secrets can be easily described as hidden, undercover, and private things done that are revealed. We all have secrets that will not be known to others concerning our life, especially past mistakes and habits displeasing to us. It is very important that we be willing to confess, confront, and let go of the secrets we have in our life, because if we don't we will cause greater harm on ourselves and could also affect the lives of others around us. I want you to know, you cannot run nor hide, whatever is done in the dark, good or evil, God is watching. In saying that, I would like to take the time to open to all who reads or shares this book with others, the secrets behind closed doors, in my life.

I began having sex at the tender age of 9 and will not blame my parents for my actions but I will say they didn't sit down and tell us the importance of not having sex at an early age. We were taught the ways of the Lord and even went through the rituals of church participation. Every Sunday, Wednesday, Friday, and also some Saturdays of the week we were in church, literally going through the motions. But when it came to the real issues of life: i.e.: how to handle finances, relationships, or personal issues, I can't remember our parents really sitting down with us in depths providing us with practical wisdom on how to handle such issues. There was so much dysfunction in the home that it brings me to tears thinking about.

Sadly my mother became a victim of her past and would always criticize our biological father and tell us things like; "Ya'll daddy is no good, he did me wrong and owe me child support!" The same typical African American woman sad song when faced with a tragic occurrence! Whether my mother realized it or not, because of her foolish talk and slandering, our minds were filled with the seed of hatred towards our biological father. This went on for nearly 15 years of our life, and sometimes may come up through conversations presently.

Our stepfather only taught us work, church, and games. Very rarely, would we see him be romantic towards our mother, and she became adept to it. Therefore I believe the physical romance between our step-dad and mother lay dormant. I truly understand what Kirk Franklin meant when he said he was taught religion but the practical ways of life he was unknowledgeable of, because I myself suffered greatly when faced with life in my early stages as an adult and even in marriage. We were rewarded for good grades in school, cleaning the house, or simply upon the mood of our parents with nearly every new game system and games. But again, what about life in general?

Being the youngest of three siblings, I was able to adapt to the pressures of life much easier than one who was maybe the only child. There were a couple of occurrences wherefore my mother and father would be at work and we would be at home alone. We were fortunate to have cable while growing up and my oldest brother was in charge of watching over us while they worked. O Oh, the windows of destruction began to swing open! Somehow my brother was able to find out the television code to watch pornography and there were even a few channels that would flash in and out with sexual scenes, and we knew it. Although at times, we were unable to vividly see the sexual scenes clearly, the enemy had planted that seed of corruption in our minds. There were times we would watch pornography for hours, not realizing what great danger we were in spiritually.

Again, I began having sex at the tender age of 9. From the age 11-18, I know I had sex with more than 60 girls (most of them were older) and never wore protection. If not sexually active with any female I would simply go over my friend house, watch pornography for hours, and masturbate uncontrollable. I had become sexually possessed, that nearly every morning and night, masturbation became my regular routine.

When I entered college, I manipulated women by singing to them and telling them foolish things like "Baby, you know I care for you a lot, and want to get to know you better!" So eventually, they became victims. Women of the church became the most collective for sexual intercourse, and I'd often hear them say crazy things like; "Oh, I'm a Christian, I don't do things like that!" It's sad how many of us today hide behind the wall of religion but secretly do sinful things, thinking that we are exempt from the judgment of God. Now back to the secrets of my life. I would sing to them or simply say things they wanted to hear, manipulating their minds we were in the bed later.

Being involved in pornography and masturbation for nearly half of my life, sexual fantasies became a seed rooted in my heart that destroyed my life. I did many ungodly acts with my ex-wife, which is totally against the commandments of God for marriage. Through those ungodly practices I was only inviting evil into our lives. I knew that I was blind to love and my heart was filtered with lust and perversion. We became trapped in a web of falsity and evil; one fantasy produces another, seducing us with sensual delights.

We must understand Jesus condemns those fantasies in which we see ourselves possessing that which we are not allowed to have. He is condemning those fantasies in which we manipulate people in our minds in ways that will appeal to and satisfy the lust of our imagination. Whether it is a forbidden partner or a forbidden sexual practice, we must be aware of the fact that the mind is capable of endless perversion.

Masturbation, in strict sense, is "sexual activity involving only one person, resulting in orgasm." Other widely used emotionally neutral terms are: *"self-stimulation," "auto-eroticism" and "self-pleasures."* Masturbation is defined in the Webster's Dictionary as "erotic stimulation involving the genital organs commonly resulting in orgasm and achieved by manual or other bodily contact exclusive of sexual intercourse, by instrumental manipulation, by sexual fantasies, or by various combinations of these agencies.

Many, who are bound to masturbation, as I was for 12 years, choose to seclude themselves in solitary. Homosexual activity is masturbation because the orgasm is obtained without regular sexual intercourse of man and woman. Oral and anal sex is a form of masturbation because it is an act of selfishness. Now the Bible doesn't mention the word masturbation, however, indirectly calls it "idolatry": sexual idolatry will damage our relationship with God and defile his temple (our bodies).

1Corinthians6:15-20

Know ye not that your bodies are the members of Christ? Shall I then take the members of Christ, and make them the members of a harlot? God forbid. What? Know ye not that he which is joined to a harlot is one body? For two, saith he, shall be one flesh. But he that is joined unto the Lord is one spirit. Flee fornication. Every sin that a man doeth is without the body; but he that committeth fornication sinneth against his own body. What? Know ye not that your body is the temple of the Holy Ghost which is in you, which ye have of God, and ye are not your own? For ye are bought with a price: therefore glorify God in your body, and in your spirit, which are God's.

A serious problem of masturbation is that it is an act of selfishness. Any sexual relation in the Bible must be an act of love in marriage, of giving yourself to the partner, and masturbation is an act of selfishness, exactly the opposite of love. When you sow love, you gather love; when you sow selfishness, you gather more selfishness. It is plain to see that masturbation is usually narcissistic and God did not design sex to be a solitary experience. It is supposed to be shared with another, and only in marriage. Masturbation can easily become a habit, and this kind of sexual selfishness is more difficult to cure than a tendency to eat too much apple pie or roast beef and potatoes.

Abstinence from sexual activity is not harmful to the body and can often be of great benefit because it allows libidinal energy to be refocused into socially redeeming activities. In the male, semen may be occasionally released spontaneously in nocturnal emissions (wet dreams), or will be slowly absorbed into the blood stream. One cannot survive without food and water, but millions of men and women live healthy, fulfilled, single lives in Christ without expressing themselves sexually.

Again, we must understand, Jesus condemns those fantasies in which we see ourselves possessing that which we are not allowed to have. He is condemning those fantasies in which we manipulate people in our minds in ways that will appeal to and satisfy the lust of our imagination. Whether it is a forbidden partner or a forbidden sexual practice, we must be aware of the fact that the mind is capable of endless perversion.

Fornication is to have sexual intercourse between two unmarried persons with the opposite sex. When one of them is married, it is Adultery. Paul uses the word fornication, porneia, in Greek, to cover all sinful sexual activity. He dealt with the problem particularly in writing the Corinthians who faced a society permeated with sexual religion and the sexual sins of a seaport. A believer must decide to be part of Christ's Body or a prostitute's body (1Corinthians 6: 12-20). The believer must flee sexual immorality and cleave to Christ, honoring him with his physical body.

Fornication is thus a result of sinful human nature (Galatians 5: 19) and unsuitable for God's holy people (Ephesians.5: 3, 1 Thess.4:3). Jesus regarded fornication as evil (Mark 7: 21), but he went against Jewish tradition and forgave prostitutes and opened the way for them to enter God's kingdom through faith (Matthew 21: 31-32, Hebrews 11:31, James 2: 25). The Book of Revelation condemns those guilty to eternal punishment, and as well as the prophets, extends the meaning of fornication to include political and religious unfaithfulness (Rev.2: 21-22, 14:8, 17:2,4, 18:3, 19:2).

Lust, Perversion, and Homosexuality

I have been tempted in the area of homosexuality throughout my whole life and have finally come to grasp of myself with the power of the Holy Ghost. The wicked and demonic strongholds of homosexuality had taken root in my heart at the age of 8 unknowingly. God had revealed to my mother that the demonic spirit of homosexuality had tried to bind me for many years and it became evident to me when I kept having run-ins with homosexuals. As a child I was very shy and small framed, and a lot of family members and friends talked about me. Due to such insults, I began to close in and shut down my emotions.

Now, my mother knew I was gifted in the aspect of singing so she put me in youth choir at the age 6. I'll be honest you, I learned how to sing in front of the crowd and even woo' a lot of adults at that age. I became very charming (cunning) and knew I could get anything I wanted from anyone, whether male or female. I won nearly all the youth competitions at school and church. Boy, I had the life any young singer would dream of! Praise, fame, and popularity, but deep down inside the spiritual wickedness of the heavens were wrecking havoc in my soul and spirit.

My mother was very keen to the spiritual world and the attacks of the enemy (and also now) and kept warning me of the homosexual spirits that had been roaming around me, but I refused to listen to her. Pride, rebellion, and ignorance of the truth nearly destroyed my life at an early age and I was unaware of it. As a youth, I was stricken medically from participating in any contact sports and would become depressed seeing all my friends in football or basketball.

My source of comfort was in girls. So I would surround myself around girls in my class and even felt a "sense" of comfort from them. "Softness" should I say! Traits such as aggressiveness, competitiveness, ambition and dominance are often regarded as masculine while traits such as kindness, sympathy, and pity are regarded as feminine.

In shame and despair, I began to exemplify more on the feminine trait rather than balance out both masculine and feminine traits. My mother later told me that a man can have all the so-called feminine traits and still be very much a man, but there must be a balance. I thought balance was in my heart; but I was more in-tune with my female friends than my male friends. Matter of a fact, I would hang around them just to have more sex with females or be introduced to their friends who were bisexual. I got involved in several sex orgies beyond measure and loved it!

The moment I received approval from medical doctors to participate in contact sports, I played. One way the spirit of homosexuality began to manifest was in athletics. There were many times I became obsessed with my own body and would walk around, desiring all eyes to be on me. I would flex and be loud but inside I was soft as tissue. Upon manifestation of those wicked spirits, I began to notice homosexuals always being around me, and I began to take liking in them. Once again, I developed a great sense of charm (cunningness) at a very young age and used it for my advantage in my years as a teen.

There were several times I would have dreams of performing anal sex upon a man or having one perform oral sex upon me until I would ejaculate. Those demonic dreams and forces would cause me to wake up in nocturnal emissions (wet dreams). While attending high school, I allowed a homosexual to perform oral sex on me and received money from him after worth. He wanted me to perform anal sex on him but I fought against it. I was so filthy and washed-out that I had begun to "secretly" (I thought) watch bisexual and homosexual pornography and masturbate to the movie. I introduced my homosexual friends to a few of my female friends who had bisexual male friends and literally watched them perform anal sex. While watching, I would masturbate and they share the pleasure of my sperm.

There was also time I were about 17 years of age, I was drunk and high, my friend and I were watching pornography literally all day. Our minds were so polluted that we wrestled and it got intense and the stronghold had weakened my body, wherefore I was no longer able to wrestle. In response to my weakness he began to perform oral sex upon me until I released on the floor.

From that moment on, I was tormented by demons for nearly 5 years, with more wicked and perverted dreams. It took the power of the Holy Ghost, to be set free from such filthy spirits and strongholds. At the age of 22, I finally made up my mind to surrender my life to Jesus and allow Him to wash my mind, heart, and soul with His Holy Blood. Jesus completely broke the sinful bonds of homosexuality, bisexuality, pride, and loneliness in my life and gave me a new heart and new mind. I am a changed man, who knows that the power of the Living God in Heaven is real and available for all!

There may be a woman who is reading this book not dating a man but rather another woman, and vise versa, a man dating another man. I will boldly say to you that such lifestyle is SIN and God is not pleased with such actions. Satan has your eyes blinded to the truth and wants you to stay in that homosexual or bisexual lifestyle, only lead to eternal damnation in hells eternal fire. There is no way anyone who stays in such lifestyle will make it to heaven according to the Word of God. God did NOT create a man to be in a sexual relationship with another man, nor did He create a woman to be in a sexual relationship with another woman.

According to the scriptures, which stands above everything I am writing, says that "it is an abomination" in the sight of God to see such things. He personally destroyed Sodom and Gomorrah for such practices, and I believe He will do likewise to anyone who continues in such heinous acts. For those who may try to excuse such actions and are supposedly of the body of Christ must be truthful with those you know in homosexual or bisexual relationship and acknowledge SIN as SIN. If we continue to go around excusing sin and watering down the Word of God, we will not inherit the kingdom of God, but be forever damned for hell punishment. There is no need to apologize for standing firm in the Word of God and the ways of God.

Again, if we are in company of someone who practices homosexuality or bisexuality and are not willing to change from their wicked and perverse ways, we must depart from them. God has commanded us to not have fellowship with darkness or evildoers. Please understand if you witness to them and they refuse to accept the Lords salvation and change their ways, God no longer holds you accountable for their souls. You are then released to move-on.

As the scriptures says in Jude 1:20-25: But ye, beloved, building up yourselves on your most holy faith, praying in the Holy Ghost, Keep yourselves in the love of God, looking for the mercy of our Lord Jesus Christ unto eternal life. And of some have compassion, making a difference: And others save with fear, pulling them out of the fire; hating even the garment spotted by the flesh. Now unto him that is able to keep you from falling, and to present you faultless before the presence of his glory with exceeding joy. To the only wise God our Savior, glory and majesty, dominion and power, both now and ever. Amen.

Again, God says that it is NOT natural for a man to lay with another man as he would lay with a woman. God also says that it is NOT natural for a woman to lay with another woman as she would lay with a man. It is an abomination to God, meaning it is disgusting to God and He hates it. So if we have His Spirit within us, we should feel the same as He does.

Any actions or relationship that are displeasing to God needs to be rooted out and destroyed, and there are steps in which you and I can take to begin the much needed process. The first thing we must do is establish a personal relationship with God by confessing our sins and having a willingness to stop doing things that are shameful to Him and others. We must have faith to believe that God came on earth through Jesus and redeemed us from sin and death, through His body on the cross at Calvary. We must also believe that Jesus is raised from the grave with all power, able to cleanse us of all unrighteousness, and is the only way to see God in heaven. Once we place our faith and life in the care of Jesus, He will dwell within us.

He is so passionate that He will never force Himself upon you. Jesus loves you so much that He will never mistreat you or leave you. He always desires to reveal Himself to you on a daily basis and promises to never leave us comfortless. He will commune with you and live in you through His Holy Spirit, upon asking. Once we have heard and believed on the Word of Truth, God seals us and opens our heart to receive His Spirit of righteousness. The many miracles Jesus Himself performed while on earth, you will be capable of doing through Him.

Again this is Gods promise to all who love Him and obey His commandments. With the leading and help of Gods Holy Spirit, you will be able to overcome any situation in life. Just know that God loves you and desires the best for your life. He is not slow to His promises and will deliver you out of any situation that is displeasing to Him if you want Him to. Trust in the Lord with all your heart my brother and sister and know that He will never fail you. Let go of any thinking or relationships that may not be benefiting you for the glory of God.

For myself, I must remind you, it took me nearly 10 years to let go of the spirit of lust and masturbation, and still at times fall short of being victorious. Yet, I have made a commitment in my heart, mind and strive daily in my actions to do what is pleasing to the Father. The moment I accepted the fact that I am no longer a slave to sin and am a servant of Christ, I drew closer to the Lord. I am continually learning daily that when we dwell in the presence of the Lord and meditate on His word, the attacks of the wicked one and troubles of the world slowly fade away.

I truly believe it is vital to be examined because the Lord is not smiling on His church. We expect the lost to run to the altar for repentance of sin and acceptance of Jesus into their life, but don't go to the altar or confess our sins to the Lord. Many of us are saved and feel that we are "holier-than-thy" and that repentance is not a part of a believers' duty. I don't believe the Lord is not looking for one who will say; "Yes, Lord, I am without sin!" but rather He is searching for those who has a contrite and humble spirit. (Isaiah 57:18) God wishes that all acknowledge their sins and become bold enough to turn away his sins. Sin leads to death, and God will not allow sinners to be in His presence. Only those who live righteous and obey His commandments can enter into the kingdom of Heaven. God doesn't hate you, yet He hates the sinful things we may continue to do.

Fortunately, he provided a way of erasing the ultimate effect of our sins, which is eternal separation from God. Our sins have eternal consequences an eternal payment for them is needed. God cannot exist directly in the presence of sin and His standards of perfection obviously could not be met by any one of us. But because He loves us so much and wants all of us to be with Him forever, He became human, suffered, and died for us to be the ultimate sacrifice for sin. That's why getting into heaven does not depend on the good things we do, it depends on whether we trust in God's payment for the debt we owe Him.

Many in the church today believe that they since they have "believed in Jesus" they can sin as much as they want or more because they are born-again sons of God that can never lose that status with Him. They have confessed Him as Lord with their mouth at some point, and now they are living pretty much as they want to.

There is no true respect for the authority of God in their lives. Some of us may actually condemn those who teach the importance of our need to be faithful to the Lord. Jesus wants our whole heart so we must be willing to confess our sins, turn away from them, allowing Him to wash and cleanse us in His blood and direct our life. If we have been sinning, or we have not been doing what God wants us to do, the answer is to turn away from our sin, and renew our love for God. God is willing to forgive - we must be willing to be changed and go in a different way.

8

Strongholds of Depression

<u>John 20:21-23 NIV</u>
Again Jesus said, "Peace be with you! As the Father has sent me, I am sending you." And with that he breathed on them and said, "Receive the Holy Spirit. If you forgive anyone his sins, they are forgiven; if you do not forgive them, they are not forgiven."

Depression is a serious problem for many people. It has many causes and thus many cures. The brain is a very complex biochemical organ, designed by God. The whole human body is so complex that many times medical science fails to properly diagnose and treat medical and emotional problems. I am not a doctor so let me insert this disclaimer here that I am not diagnosing or treating any one by the information provided. Now your decision on how to treat your health is between you and God and your physician.

I believe in seeking the advice of physicians for health problems and I believe that God sometimes gives physicians wisdom on treating people. There are also times when physicians do not have all of the answers, and medical science can only do so much. The information I am providing here is from my own experience and observations, and what I believe are some of the things that the Bible says about depression. Adding to the complexity of mental illnesses is the fact that people have a spirit, a soul, and they live in a physical body.

Depression can have a physical cause, an emotional cause, or be a spiritual condition, or any combination of all three. Once depression sets in it seems to then affect all areas of ones life, bringing down the total person into a depressed state of being. Many things can trigger depression such as, a relationship gone badly, a physical problem, or a spiritual problem, which usually involves the person not trusting God because they don't know how much God loves them.

A person can be a shinning star radiating love and light outward toward others, then something will trigger depression and the person becomes a black hole in which light and love cannot escape. Everything is sucked into it and it is never satisfied it seeks help from people, help from chemicals, help from everyone and everything.

Sometimes there is temporary relief, but eventually everything succumbs to the power of the black hole, the wrong quick fixes cause the hole to become bigger and with more power, as hopelessness increases like the power of gravity when matter is added to the black hole. Other people try to help and encourage the depressed person, but eventually they feel themselves being sucked into the black hole so they begin to pull away and avoid the situation.

There is only one person that gives out more light and love than a black hole can absorb; His name is Jesus and He can cure all depression weather it has physical, mental, or spiritual causes. His Love and Power are far greater than the power of your black hole. What I am about to say may sound harsh but it is from my own experience.

Sometimes people don't want to be cured from depression because it has become their identity, and they are afraid that without it they would be nobody. They have come to believe that is who they are. But that is not who you are and God has a plan and a purpose for your life, if you choose to seek it, you will find it. God has made you in His image, and you are unique from everyone else on earth, only you can fulfill the destiny that God has planned for you.

Jeremiah29:11-13NIV
For I know the plans I have for you, declares the LORD, plans to prosper you and not to harm you, plans to give you hope and a future. Then you will call upon me and come and pray to me, and I will listen to you. You will seek me and find me when you seek me with all your heart.

If you reject the Love of God and choose to put your hope and faith in the "right pill", the "right person", or the "right circumstance" to find your happiness then you should be depressed. Because you have rejected the one who really loves you, the one who is your Hope, and your Life, the One who is your source of Joy. David wrote about his depression, (Psalms 43:5) why am I discouraged? Why so sad? I will put my hope in God! I will praise him again-- my Savior and my God! David knew who is hope was.

Many people in the Bible had bouts with depression and their lessons are recorded as examples for us. David wrote about his depression many times in the book of Psalms. Psalms is an excellent book to read for encouragement.

If you are depressed because of rejection, sorrow, grief, or physical suffering; give those things to Jesus because He already carried them to the cross for you. He knows your pain and He already suffered your agony so that He could replace them with His peace and healing He offers you.

We must always remember who the source of our help is. God may use physicians and give them the wisdom to treat you, He may use other people and even circumstances, but ultimately our help comes from God. So always seek help from God first and then being guided by the Holy Spirit obeys His voice and His word. No matter how God does it every good thing comes down from our Father in heaven. Always give God the thanks, and praise, and the glory. When we turn to the Lord and ask Him for His Holy Spirit He promises to give it. A root of bitterness can grow up in a person due to unforgiveness causing sever depression. Sometimes people do and say things that hurt us very deeply.

Ephesians 4:26-27 NKJV
"Be angry, and do not sin": do not let the sun go down on your wrath, nor give place to the devil.

Hebrews 12:14-15 NIV
Make every effort to live in peace with all men and to be holy; without holiness no one will see the Lord. See to it that no one misses the grace of God and that no bitter root grows up to cause trouble and defile many.

How to know if you have truly forgiven someone that has hurt you. Do you say or think things like this? I forgive the person but I will let God deal with them. If you want God to judge and punish them, that is not forgiveness. Do you say things like, I forgive the person but I do not want to see them or talk to them again? How would you feel if God said to you I forgive you but I am going to avoid you and not speak to you, would you feel forgiven? That is not forgiveness. God's forgiveness always restores.

Do you still have any anger or bad feelings toward the person? When you fully forgive the person, anger will be replaced with pity for them. Do you still hold on to the memory of the wrong done to you thinking about it often? True forgiveness forgets, because of the healing of forgiveness the pain disappears as if it did not happen.

When God forgives He forgets it forever as if it never occurred. Do you have trouble accepting God's love for you? If so it could be because you are standing in judgment of another person, because you don't have mercy, it is hard for you to believe that God has mercy and compassion for you. Part of the meaning of the word blessed means to be happy, joyful, and depression free.

Sometimes we may think that we have forgiven someone but we really have not. When you fully forgive, God's peace will rest upon you, and the Holy Spirit will comfort you. This is how to enter into the healing forgiveness, compassion, mercy, and Love of God, which is His grace. Get on your knees and enter into prayer for the person that has hurt you. Approach the throne of grace, in front of the mercy seat, and petition your Father in heaven to please forgive this person. Ask God almighty to pour out His grace, mercy, and compassion upon this person, and in this person.

Whether we acknowledge this or not; depression may lead to suicide, since it is precisely despair that is the forerunner of this terrible act. Suicide is the willing deprivation of one's life. Some people with bipolar disorder become suicidal. Anyone who is thinking about committing suicide needs immediate attention, preferably from a mental health professional or a physician. Anyone who talks about suicide should be taken seriously. Risk for suicide appears to be higher earlier in the course of the illness. Therefore, recognizing bipolar disorder early and learning how best to manage it may decrease the risk of death by suicide. Signs and symptoms that may accompany suicidal feelings include:

1. talking about feeling suicidal or wanting to die
2. feeling hopeless, that nothing will ever change
3. feeling like a burden to family and friends
4. abusing alcohol or drugs

If you are feeling suicidal or know someone who is:

1. call a doctor, emergency room, or 911 right away, get immediate help
2. make sure you, or the suicidal person, are not left alone
3. Make sure that access is prevented to large amounts of medication, weapons, or other items that could be used for self-harm.

      While some suicide attempts are carefully planned over time, others are impulsive acts that have not been well thought out; thus, the final point in the box above may be a valuable long-term strategy for people with bipolar disorder. Either way, it is important to understand that suicidal feelings and actions are symptoms of an illness that can be treated. With proper treatment, suicidal feelings can be overcome.

      In the United States, a person dies by suicide every 16 minutes, claiming more than 32,000 lives each year. It is estimated that an attempt is made every minute: with close to one million people attempting suicide annually. Suicide is the forth leading cause of death in the U.S. among adults 18-65, the third leading cause of death among teens and young adults, and individuals ages 65 and older account for 16 percent of all suicide deaths.

      Before one commits suicide, many have no idea that there stands a vile, inexpressibly evil spirit behind their backs, urging them to kill the body, break the precious "clay vessel" protecting the soul until God's set time. And this spirit suggests, and urges, and demands, and compels, and frightens with all sorts of fears: only in order that a person would press the trigger or jump over the windowsill, running away from life, from his unbearable anguish... The Sixth Commandment states, "Thy shall not kill" (Ex. 20:13; Deut. 5:17).

Notice, there is no distinction made between killing another person and killing oneself. A person considering suicide has reached that point by allowing circumstances in his life to rule over him. The apostle Paul asked, "Know you not, that to whom you yield yourselves servants to obey, his servants you are to whom you obey; whether of sin unto death, or of obedience unto righteousness?" (Rom. 6:16).

In verse 12, he exhorts us, "Let not sin therefore reign in your mortal body, that you should obey it in the lusts thereof." In Matthew 22:39, Christ taught, "... You shall love your neighbor *as* yourself. " In Ephesians 5:29, Paul stated, "For no man ever yet hated his own flesh; but nourishes and cherishes it... " A person contemplating suicide may say that he hates himself, but his real motivation is one of utter self-love, to the point that he totally disregards the feelings and needs of others, and the impact that his actions will have on his family and friends.

Suicide is a national health problem and demonic stronghold that must be acknowledged and conquered by the power of God. Those who commit suicide receive the same judgment as those who do not even believe God's Word. Their ultimate reward is shown in Revelation 21:8: "But the fearful, and unbelieving, and the abominable, and murderers, and whoremongers, and sorcerers, and idolaters, and all liars, shall have their part in the lake which burns with fire and brimstone: which is the second death." The Bible clearly shows that the unpardonable sin is any sin not repented of (Heb. 10:26; I John 5:16; Jas. 4:17). Killing is plainly sin. One who kills himself will not be excused from the punishment of hell.

9

Silence of Abuse

2 Timothy 1-5
Know this also, that in the last days perilous times shall come. For men shall be lovers of their own selves, covetous, boasters, proud, blasphemers, disobedient to parents, unthankful, unholy, without natural affection, trucebreakers, false accusers, incontinent, **fierce**, despisers of those that are good, traitors, heady, high-minded, lovers of pleasures more than lovers of God; Having a form of godliness but denying the power thereof: from such turn away.

We live in a society where many relationships are failing. Abuse is rampant, but we don't know what to do about it. In fact, many people dismiss it as normal because it is something that they grew up with in their home as a child. Do we get into such relationships because we are poor at choosing a compatible partner, or more to the point, do we not know what signs to look for that would indicate that something is wrong or will be soon.

Abuse in its different manifestations is the most destructive tool that can be used by anyone against another person. It is designed to distort a person's view of self, reality and of God, thus keeping that person from having a fruitful life. It is a CONTROL spirit and can cause many to become adapt to such poison.

When there is abuse going on in a relationship, it's time to separate. It doesn't matter how holy or good the person seems, who is doing the violating. There are different types of abuse and they are all designed for one thing and one thing only, DESTRUCTION! I believe all types of abuse can be put into one of these categories:

PhysicalAbuse: which is body torture that is used to subdue and control another person.

SexualAbuse: torturing both a person physically and emotionally using unlawful sex acts as the weapon, i.e. prostitution, adultery, incest, homosexuality, rape, marriage rape, anything immoral or illegal sexually.

VerbalAbuse: designed to distort the truth a person holds about something or someone, in order to gain control over someone's mind.

SpiritualAbuse: used to manipulate another person to serve any other god than Jesus while many times exalting the abuser. At its worse, satanic ritual abuse, which, many times include all the other categories of abuse. There is also a form of spiritual abuse, wherefore the man of the house may spend more time in the churches preaching than at home, caring for their family. I know and have known many leaders who choose to fill their schedule with conferences and seminars, travel around the world, but not even set aside time for his family.

Sadly, all these types of abuses deeply scar the emotions of a person and usually greatly alter their perception and their ability to live life to its fullest. But there is hope and it lies in Jesus. He has come to heal the broken-hearted. If you have been abused and are hurt deeply inside, there is hope, healing, and full restoration. If you will yield your heart to the Holy Spirit sent from God to be our helper, He will lead you through every traumatic situation that you have been through into wholeness. The process is painful.
However, on the other side of each "door of pain" is a place of joy, peace, and rest.

You must diligently give yourself to study of the Bible daily, turn your ears and eyes away from the TV, radio, movies, books and the like, and turn all of your heart over to Jesus; He will tenderly minister life to you instead of death. Share the pain of your heart with Him while searching the Scriptures for the answers. As you do these things you will gradually and continually become a whole, hurt-free, peaceful, and joyful person. You will even start to like yourself. And how good that will feel!

First and foremost I must admit to all, there are **NO EXCUSES** for abuse, therefore the results and consequences for ones" violent act should be punishable for jail. When one abuse, he or she violates ones freedom to be themselves, and everyone become affected by the results. Abusers are deemed in society as predators and only cause shame upon their own lives when their actions are exposed. Again, I must admit and boldly say to all abuse or know one who abuse; there are **NO EXCUSES** for abuse, and I guarantee you that eventually you will be arrested for such actions.

I cannot proceed any further without being honest in my actions, which lead to divorce in marriage. Early stages in my life revealed to everyone including myself that I had struggled with self-esteem, therefore I would go from woman to woman seeking soul satisfaction. While dating my ex-wife everything was well, yet there were errors in my personal life and I lacked wisdom or the "know-how" to put under subjection, and looked to everyone else except Jesus for help.

    I resided with my brother after being released from jail and knew that my life had been restored. My brother kept me encouraged and literally would do anything for me, to assist in my restoration and growth both physically and spiritually, yet I took advantage of his kindness and allowed pride to creep in my heart. I was only asked to pay half on rent and if I could, pay half on the utilities, but I would take my checks and spend it on music equipment, so when rent time came around I would always make excuses and only pay about ¼ of the rent.

    I did not live up to my obligation and only caused shame in my life. I eventually met my ex wife and we began dating and my brother noticed I was spending on her but when it came down to contributing to the expenses at home, I would always come up short, so one morning, he told me to leave and stay with my girlfriend, since I was always with her anyways. So I left in anger not realizing that I opened the door of my heart to demonic strongholds, therefore, I carried demonic spirits with me everywhere I had gone.

    Knowing that I had been foolish in my actions when my brother opened his heart and door to help me, I went through depression, which led to traumatic events of suicide. I would look in the mirror and say to myself, *"I hate you; you are worthless, and wish I would just die now!"* This became normal in my daily communication wherefore I constipated suicide three times in one week. Everyone became my enemy, including my ex wife. When she would simply ask me, *"Myron what is going on?"* I would literally lash out at her or push her away from me.

    There was one occurrence where I had come in from work and noticed she went through my property but she said she only looked at the stuff not fondled through it, so instead of me accepting the truth of what she was saying (shameful, because I had some playboy magazines in there that she may have noticed) I grabbed her arm and slapped her. Immediately, she ran away from me and left. But came back later and told me to get my stuff and leave but I refused. Knowing that fear was in her heart towards me, I embraced her and lied, saying I would not do it again but only to keep from being homeless again.

I manipulated her in such a way that if I would frown, she would get scared, but all alone I was afraid of her. God began to show His mercy towards me, by allowing me to meet a well-known counselor and musician, and he identified those spirits within me and had even provided me with counseling at no cost encouraging me not to be involved in any relationship until I had renounced those demonic spirits and allow the Lord to cleanse me. I began to work with him in many of his business endeavors and he provided wise counsel to me on a daily basis. *"Man, I was living the life!"* Yet deep down inside, I still allowed the satanic force to hide within, that's why I know the scriptures are true.

<u>Matthew12:43-45</u>
*"When an evil spirit comes out of a man, it goes through arid places seeking rest and does not find it. Then it says, "I will return to the house I left." When it arrives, it finds the house unoccupied, swept clean and put in order. Then it goes and takes with it **seven** other spirits wicked than itself and they go in and live there. And the final condition of that man is **worse** than the first.*

I became demon possessed and lurked for more trouble from my ex-wife and everyone else, so when she challenged my beliefs or the beliefs of others I would abuse, and laugh while abusing whether verbally or physically. This went on continually for at least two years in dating, but I hide my actions from her family and my family until we received marital counseling from her parents in hopes of controlling her not loving her. I told them that I had abused her and would not abuse her again so they believed that I was honest and months later proceeded with the marriage ceremony.

Now we openly refused counseling from our pastors as a couple, because we knew the secrets behind closed doors would be exposed. We didn't love one another because first of all, love does <u>not</u> abuse and secondly, fear is a demonic stronghold, which can only be rooted out by the power of the Holy Ghost. So in marriage we did not go through a dry-spell "honeymoon."

We literally continued in the steps of destruction knowingly.

There was one last event of my outrageous abuse towards her on August 03, 2007, wherefore we planned an event to go out to dinner yet the schedule was changed and I got upset and expressed it to her sexually by being aggressive with her and not allowing her to enjoy herself. It was all about me... *"Yeah Myron, go get it, get it, get it boy! Pay her back for letting you down, and break her off a lil' something, something!"*

Those were all the words that I heard the demons replay in my head! So I thought I was representing! Until I looked at her through the eyes of God: it was as though God showed me how she was at that moment: **DEAD** without hope. When I looked at her she was also crying with no expression and I knew she had been damaged inside both physically and spiritually. Then she gracefully said, *"Myron, I love you! Why did you do this to me?"*

The shame and pain that goes through my heart now, just remembering what I had done to Gods precious daughter causes me to cry often, as I type my testimony to the world. I violated my own wife verbally, physically, and spiritually, and confess to the world that I too, Myron DeShun Banks, am a sinner only saved by Gods grace, deserving the full extent of His wrath, because my works were void and my ways were truly displeasing to God.

I dare not put myself on a pedestal or try to hold any foolish title because all that means nothing to God. It's all about how you love Him and treat your neighbor, whom you see everyday. I can honestly admit I had no respect or love for God, my neighbor, or myself and was doomed for hell eternally because of my acts of violence.

From my actions alone, I know God never commands a woman to stay in situations where she or her child is physically in danger. It is not mans' rightful place or authority to abuse a woman whether they are dating or under a marital covenant. If he physically abuses you, he has overstepped the bounds of love and you must leave such situation with the help of others. If you have children, remember that you are the only protection they have. It takes courage and commitment to God to remove yourself and your family from a situation where you are in physical danger.

But with God's help you can do it. God's word does not directly address the matter of physical abuse in marriage. Therefore many leaders of the church organization will not teach about marital covenant roles and accountability. I truly believe such lack of communication of the realness of abuse in marriage within the church, contributes to a record high account of divorce.

Verbal abuse is a very touchy subject with women and with psychologists. Most seem to advocate that a wife should never tolerate it. I agree. If mere tolerance is her attitude, she is allowing great harm to be done to herself. There are also the children to consider. If they are being verbally abused, a mother must remember that she is the only protection her children have. She is the one who must make choices to safeguard their well-being. Verbal abuse has the same potential to cause injury that physical abuse does.

Verbal abuse causes severe psychological damage to some. However, I do not believe it always has to damage us. I believe God can use it to strengthen us and help us conform to the image of Jesus. We are commanded to "Be imitators of God, therefore, as dearly loved children" (Ephesians 5:1).

Could it be possible that the verbal abuse some women experience is God's way of working things for good in our lives that we may be refined by the fire and proved genuine to the praise and glory of our Lord Jesus Christ? Could it be that he wants to use the abusive situation to teach us the same tender compassion for the abuser that Jesus displayed? Could it be that he wants to strengthen our hearts so that we can learn to have peace amidst every circumstance as we rest in him?

I cannot with good conscience advocate that women must leave their husbands just because they experience verbal abuse. Yet I realize that some are not able or ready to go through verbally abusive situations without being damaged themselves. I believe God understands this.

So my position on the matter of verbal abuse is that a woman should step back and consider what is at stake. She should seek counsel and help from others whom she can trust. But most of all she should ask the Lord Jesus to direct her steps and show her what his plan for her is at this moment.

    Again for anyone who is in an abusive relationship, I would like to encourage you to get out of it. Seek counseling, and petition to the Lord your hurt and pains. The Lord will guide you in the path of righteousness; alongside protect you all the way through your life. No one deserves to be abused. If you are guilty of abusing someone, I encourage you to give up those sinful deeds, repent to Jesus, surrender your life to Him, and allow Him to guide you in all your ways. Abuse is not pleasurable in the sight of those who are abused, or God, so I encourage you to allow love to rest, rule, and abide in your heart daily and free yourself from that bondage of torment.

10

RED ALERT: *Cycle of Abuse*

2 Timothy 1-5

Know this also, that in the last days perilous times shall come. For men shall be lovers of their own selves, covetous, boasters, proud, blasphemers, disobedient to parents, unthankful, unholy, without natural affection, trucebreakers, false accusers, incontinent, **fierce**, despisers of those that are good, traitors, heady, high-minded, lovers of pleasures more than lovers of God; having a form of godliness but denying the power thereof: from such turn away.

As stated in Chapter 9, abuse is an ever growing epidemic in society and a true sign of the end of age. In 2 Timothy 3:1-4 Paul forewarns Timothy about the terrible times to come when many forms of wickedness will characterize the godless people he should avoid, saying there will be terrible times in the last days. People will be lovers of themselves, lovers of money, boastful, proud, **abusive**, disobedient to their parents, ungrateful, unholy, without love, unforgiving, slanderous, **without self-control**, brutal, not lovers of the good, treacherous, rash, conceited, lovers of pleasure rather than lovers of God- having a form of godliness but denying its power. Have nothing to do with them.

Not only was this scripture for Timothy but also for us. We must take the Word of God as it is and apply the principals to our lives on a daily basis. Jesus clearly said that He will not judge us but His Word shall judge us, and His Word is above His name. There will be no excuses in judgment when we each stand before God giving account for all deeds done in the body whether good or evil.

The moment we have come into the knowledge of the truth and the Word of God, our heart and lives has been marked for judgment. Scriptures says it is appointed unto man after death, judgment! Therefore my brothers and sisters, take notice, the Lord is watching everything we do whether good or evil. Every secret thing done in the dark shall be brought into the light, and guess what? God is the light of the world and nothing secret shall escape His dreadful presence.

As I also stated in Chapter 9, there are **NO EXCUSES** for abuse. Now there are some demonic forces that enter into a man or woman who chose to abuse. Usually if one witnessed abuse of any form as a child, statistically he or she is more likely to become an abuser if the demonic spirits are not cast out of their heart. The demonic spirit of anger, pain, and bitterness, has to come to root at one moment in the person, but how they handle it is the question. I stated "demonic spirit" because we know we wrestle not against flesh and blood but against spiritual wickedness and rulers of the darkness.

We must be willing to educate our children, love ones, and friends of the dangers of abuse and the harsh consequences that follow for such heinous crime. Whether male or female, there are no reasons you should allow yourself to be a victim of abuse or should you abuse.

It is no coincidence that an overwhelming majority of the victims of domestic violence and sexual assault are women and children. However, men are not the only ones in our society who use violence. Women and children are becoming more violent as well, oftentimes responding to acts of violence with violence. Again there are many factors, such as alcohol and drug use and poverty, contribute to a growing use of violence. But there are NO EXCUSES!

While attending counseling, I've learned there are mainly 3 stages to the Cycle of Violence: Tension Building Stage, the Violent Episode, and the Honeymoon Stage. Domestic violence increases in frequency and severity. It is never an isolated incident or a one-time occurrence. I would like to provide a vital breakdown of the three stages of the cycle of violence; I have been privileged to learn while receiving my breakthrough from such heinous crime.

HoneymoonStage: This is where violent relationships often begin. The abuser is charming, caring, gentle and affectionate. He or she may present their victim with gifts, go out of their way to do nice things for them, and generally make their victim feel accepted and loved.

TensionBuildingStage: According to Walker, acts of violence are generally preceded by periods of growing unrest within the relationship. The abuser may become increasingly jealous, short tempered or paranoid. The victim will often try to protect his or her self by placating the abuser.

Unfortunately, an abusive person's anger is often irrational and therefore cannot be reasonably calmed. In many relationships, there is nothing the victim can do to avoid upsetting their partner.

ViolentAbuse: This is when things come to a head and the abuser becomes violent. In addition to physical attacks, a batter might use threats, intimidating behavior and emotional abuse to keep his or her victim in line. During this phase, victims are often too frightened to seek out help.

Abusers can vary widely in their behavior, motivations and tactics. There are many different ways that a person can be manipulated. Some abusers rely mostly on emotional or verbal abuse, rarely if using physical attacks. I also believe the characteristics of the individual, family, social situation, and community may be related to which men are violent or may become violent. The emotional and psychological characteristics are influenced by family structure and situations. The breakdown of a man's "power" may lead to violence in the home.

When a man feels powerless and tries to regain control of his masculine image, he may become forceful in any manner possible. Power is never to be forced upon anyone and if so, that person is literally weak as a feather.

Many men fear appearing feminine so he might walk around with an "image" that he is all powerful and in control of situations. Many have outburst of rage, loud speaking, criticize another male, or simply do a lot of extracurricular activities. I tell you the truth, such men as I were, are able to be broken and there is no need to fear, because ultimately such men fear you. When women stand up for righteousness and not tolerate abuse, fear grips that perpetrators heart and mind.

As I stated in my testimony of abusing my ex-wife, although I appeared masculine, I was soft as tissue, and in my heart, all alone I was afraid of her. I believe many men abuse due to low-self esteem, for the protection and assurance of not being portrayed as a homosexual or "soft."

Although there are no excuses for abusing, many who abuse have been abused themselves physically, emotionally, or sexually, and felt a sense of unworthiness in society or around their family. Usually such actions may cause him to doubt himself as being masculine or feminine at one moment in his life, even to the point of constipating suicide, as myself.

There was one moment in counseling my therapist challenged my belief and I burst out in rage and she simply looked me in the dept of my eyes and said; "Myron, you are <u>not</u> what you did! Sit down and accept "change!" The moment she boldly proclaimed that, my heart was broken and the wall of shame, guilt, and anger, was torn down. The peace and joy of God filled my heart and I began to feel confident in myself, knowing I am no longer held captive to the demonic stronghold of abuse. I made a vow in my heart and charged accountability from family, friends, and co-workers, to continue to pray with and for me and watch my actions.

I had to stop abusing myself first. It took a lot of diligent work and accountability from others to move forward and not return back to such vomit. Scriptures says in Proverbs 26:11 as a dog returns back to its vomit so a fool repeats his folly and in Matthew 12:45 the evil spirit comes back and takes with it **seven** other spirits wicked than itself and enters the mans spirit and the final condition of that man is **worse** than the first.

There is no need to continue on sinning. God is merciful but in His mercy He must recompense us rightfully for our works. The wages of sin is death and before one dies, usually there is a phase of suffering. If there be any suffering, as scriptures say, "let it be for righteousness sake."

My brothers and sisters, God is willing and able to free you from any cycle of abuse and restore unto you the joy of your youth. I encourage you to accept change in your life by first acknowledging your sinful behavior, confessing them to Jesus Christ, believing that He is able to forgive you of sins, and finally allowing Him to rule and guide your life from this moment forth.

Don't be as Lot's wife; God commanded them to leave Sodom because His judgment and wrath had been ignited against the land due to their sins, but she looked back and become a pillar of salt. Figuratively speaking she became of no existence and likewise shall anyone be if they chose to continue in such destructive ways.

11

Mended but Broken

Galatians 6:7-8
Be not deceived: God is not mocked: for whatsoever a man soweth, that shall he also reap. For he that soweth to his flesh shall reap corruption: but he that soweth to the Spirit shall the Spirit reap life everlasting.

My life consisted of many ups and downs and the seeds I had planted prior to me marrying my ex-wife began to take root early in marriage. Suffering from low self esteem, anger, and bitterness, I lived a life full of falsehood for the extent of 6 years in knowing my ex wife, but tried to cover it through the rituals of church going. I was counted as a church favorite amongst the young adults due to being a gospel recording artist and mentor to the youth but darkness filled my heart. I'd attend church on a regular basis: Wednesday night youth bible study, Thursday night prayer meeting, Saturday morning choir meeting, and of course Sunday morning worship.

I was truly living the life! Beyond church activities, I would travel the state on a monthly basis singing my heart out to the crowd but never dealt with the issues I held secretly in me heart (*at least I thought secretly*) before I go any further, I would like to say that the eyes of the Lord are everywhere watching both the good and the evil we may do and whatever a man sow in his life that must he reap. Therefore we can't continue on blaming others for our wrongful actions. We may have been influenced by someone or demonic activities but still the choice was ultimately up to us to make.

In knowing I was very cunning and sexually advanced in relation to me ex, I groomed her by playing the role of a little child around her. Anything she wanted done I did (cleaning, cooking, romancing her, writing her songs, helping her mother and grandmother). I literally remember a moment she and I had got into an argument and my mentor came by to talk with us. In the midst of the conversation, I manipulated her by stating I was going to leave her; she began to cry and begged me to stay,
"Myron, I'll do whatever, to please you!!"

From that moment on, I knew I held her captive as my prisoner and there was no way she would be able to leave me except though death. My mentor told me when she said such statement, he seen a demonic spirit arise and show its face. He encouraged me to leave her and get me life right with the Lord because I had been demonic influenced and on a path to destruction. Yet, I brushed off his words of wisdom and stayed with her.

From that moment on, I began to lose weight and anger filled my heart towards her but while attending church functions or around family I'd act as though everything was fine. I'd shout halleluiah, praise the Lord, thank you Jesus (*as a form of mockery*) to camouflage my true identity. Boy, did I have them all! Even my wife thought I was being delivered and set free until... we arrived home. Just at the spear of a moment after church, I threaten her often by telling her, *"If you tell anyone I am abusing you I will kill you! You belong to me and you owe me your life, just remember what you said _ _ _ _ _!"*

Now there were times when we were intimate and I would literally block her out of my mind and think of other women and have my way with her, leave her curled up on the bed crying. Knowing she was damaged both physically, spiritually and mentally the little boy in me (rather should I say) my truly emotions would wrestle with the demonic forces. There were times I would cry and literally hear the demons say to me, *"Toughen up you belong to us! Your soul is ours, ha, ha, ha, she deserved it!!"*

I used control and power by buying her gifts after an argument (the gifts I wanted her to have not what she particularly wanted). And if someone outside of me would give her gifts I would get upset and take the gifts from her. I tell you the truth, I lived a life truly displeasing unto God and many of my acquaintances didn't comprehend it. I was lost in my ways possessing a form of godliness but lacking the power of God to be free from such path of destruction.

Although I did not encounter sexually with another woman I was still unfaithful towards my ex-wife because I didn't love her outwardly as I know I should have. I said I loved her but my actions were contrary and I lived a double life that resulted in much heartache I currently endure now, and I can not say it is for righteousness sake. For he that soweth to his flesh shall reap corruption. I sowed seeds of unrighteousness for nearly 7 years towards her and now the fruits are blossoming.

When our pastors saw the evidence of abuse upon her, I was immediately banned from attending the church organization. After 6 long dreadful years, my true identity was exposed! A double minded man who was truly unstable in all his ways!! I will not blame her for any of the situations I may currently face due to my heinous actions because I will say that she was a great wife and deserved to be free from me. I have decided to change my actions and receive the much needed counseling for my actions and have come to realization that I, Myron DeShun Banks have been mended yet still feel broken!

12

The Enemy IN ME
"SELF DESTRUCTION"

<u>Mark 5:1-5</u>
And they came over unto the other side of the sea, into the country of the Gadarenes. And when He was come out of the ship, immediately there met him out of the tombs a man with an unclean spirit, Who had his dwelling among the tombs; and no man could bind him, no, not with chains: Because that he had been often bound with fetters and chains, and the chains had been plucked asunder by him, and the fetters broken in pieces: neither could any man tame him. And always, night and day, he was in the mountains, and in the tombs, crying, and **cutting himself** with stones.

Now there may be a few readers who may not have encountered abuse from another individual and the perpetrator may surprisingly be "SELF." Quite often, abuse is spoken of as harming someone else, but not many consider self-abuse. Again, abuse is defined as any thing that is harmful, injurious, or offensive or improper treatment. Abuse also includes excessive and wrongful misuse of anything.

There is a story in the Holy Word of God in Mark 5:1-20, wherefore Jesus and his disciples made it to shore from a very weary storm on the sea. Jesus must have been very tired because He was sleeping in the stern of the boat. He was awaken' because His followers lacked faith that they He gave them power to calm the winds. Just image how He felt at that moment. He ministered all day long and may have not ate much, and just wanted to rest. I just got a vivid illustration of Him frowning fiercely at His disciples in disgust, wondering "why did ya'll wake me up for this crap, man I was in la, la, land?" And I'm pretty sure He felt like we do at times and said to His disciples "Man, I'm sick of dealing with ya'll, where is ya'll faith? Can a brother get some sleep around here?"

Well just imagine yourself, sleeping and snoring in "la, la land." But suddenly you were awaken by your children or someone dear to you and asked to do something they were capable of doing. Lets' be real, how would you feel? Hold on, before anyone answers that question, there are some reading this that need to pull down the wall of religion and answer this question with truth. If you're truthful in your heart, you will boldly answer, "I would be upset!" Not only would you be upset but also you might even say a word or two that would hurt that person feeling.

Well, Jesus carried the same emotions we carried, so don't water down His Word as though He was all calm and full of joy at that moment! And I'm quite sure He was unable to go back to sleep due to frustration and them rejoicing and saying "What manner of man is this that at His command even the wind and storms obey Him?"

Now when they made it to shore, the first thing Jesus saw was a man possessed with demons, cutting himself with stones. Can you imagine also, Jesus being exhausted and tired, rubbing His eyes as they got off the boat and in a blurred view, seeing that man cutting himself and screaming? Man, I wish I were there to see the look on His face! Real talk, it had to a strange look like; "I know I ain't tripping or seeing things, but what the heck is up with that man cutting himself and screaming out loud disturbing these folks? He must be crazy!"

I would like to get back on point with the subject of "self destruction." Consider this my friend, we may at any period of time in our life, been like unto the man filled with demons cutting himself' with stones. I like to let you know, there are many ways we may be inflicting harm upon ourselves; physically, mentally, emotionally, or spiritually and not know it until some else recognize those demonic strongholds. Do you abuse yourself? Do you sleep late, work late, eat junk, neglect your body, and worry excessively? Do you find it hard to get out of the trap you've got yourself into? Do you find you are swimming in a mire of quicksand unable to get out? Do you find you have gotten weary and disillusioned with life? Again, you must understand physical, mental, emotional, and spiritual abuse is harmful:

Do you abuse your physical life? Do you put poison in your body? Do you drink excessively, smoke, or take excessive medication or drugs? Do you eat excessively? Do you deprive your body of having enough sleep and rest? Do you work your body so hard that it doesn't have a chance to recover?

Do you deprive yourself of recreation? If so, I will let you know this is **physical** abuse. Do you think the same thoughts over again? Do you deprive yourself of expanding your horizons, learning a new skill? Are you trapped in the same old way of thinking and deprive yourself of the adventure of expanding your horizons?

If you don't use your mind, you lose it. Do you deprive yourself of mental breaks? Do you have too much mental break and do not exercise your mind enough? Do you take time to dream or do you dream excessively and do not put into action? If so, this is **mental** abuse.

Do you abuse your emotional life? Do you tell yourself you're no good, worry unnecessarily, or think negative thoughts? Do you bear grudges, harbor anger, doubt, guilt, and regrets? Do you harbor unforgiveness towards yourself or someone else? Do you hold grudges and magnify them? Do you beat yourself up when something goes wrong, and blame yourself excessively? Do you blame others excessively something goes wrong? If so, my friend, this is **emotional** abuse.

Do you abuse your personal life? Do you form bad habits that are hard to break? Do you find yourself drawn to these bad habits over and over again and cannot help yourself? Do you sabotage yourself? Do you work very had for something and when it is near to success, back away? Do you deprive yourself of the things you want to do?

Have you lost the capacity for enjoyment, that even if you had a million dollars or the environment is right, you are not able to enjoy? Do you harden yourself against the wonder and beauty of the world? Do you alienate from the love, goodness of God and refuse to come into the knowledge of Him through a personal relationship with Him? If so, my friend, this is **spiritual** abuse.

I'm willing to let you know there are not only consequences for abusing someone else but there are also consequences for abusing yourself. At any moment you could encounter an early death with great pain and suffering. Mentally you would continue suffering and deprived of the joy God has for all who would receive and act upon. There are many who I have known that carried around diseases, bitterness, hurt, unforgiveness and grudges. As a result has either committed suicide or died of a heart attack. Is this how you want to live?

Remember my brothers and sisters; there is still power in the mighty name of Jesus. There is no force of darkness that can stand against Him for our Lord holds all power in His hands and has defeated all the works of Satan on the cross through His body. He alone has overcome sin and death therefore through Him we may overcome sin and death.

Jesus of Nazareth walked this earth in fullness of Gods power, and the demons knew that when they encountered Him, they would be cast out because their powers were matchless in comparison to God. Again, Jesus walked out of the boat after calming the winds and saw a man possessed with demons. Immediately the demons cried out, "What have I to do with thee, Jesus, thou Son of the Most High God? I adjure thee by God, that thou torment me not!"

The demons begged Jesus not to inflict harm upon them but rather allow them to reside in the body of a swine. How interesting such statement is! After careful prayer and studying of such scriptures, I've come to realization that the forces of darkness are powerless when not in a dwelling place. Their torment includes also being absent from a body to dwell in. It's like they lose strength and become very fearful at that moment cast out of a person, because they have no hiding place or should I say place to exercise their craft of wickedness. Secondly, demons only like to reside in anything filthy and unclean whether it is a nasty house or body; figuratively speaking filthy conscience.

Through the power of the Holy Ghost, we have power over all the works of Satan. As Disciples of Christ, we have been given power of the Holy Ghost, therefore when the rulers of darkness see us they should tremble at our presence because of Gods' Holy Spirit dwelling in us.

There is no reason for us to fear the forces of darkness if Jesus is our Lord. Will you allow the enemy to defeat you with fear or will you defeat the enemy with the sword of the spirit, which is the Word of God? Jesus said in Luke 10:19; "Behold, I give unto you power to tread on serpents and scorpions, and over all the power of the enemy: and nothing shall by any means hurt you."

When faced with an opposition, lift up your voice unto God with praise and thanksgiving, knowing you have victory. All the rulers of darkness become confused when we praise and worship the Lord instead of meditating on our problems. We must also remind the enemy that he is defeated and has no power over our lives. Jesus came that we might have life and enjoy life in abundance of joy. The joy of the Lord is our strength and the joys that He gives can no man take away nor can be described.

If you truly want to be free from the ways that leads to destruction, you must be like the man in the above passage. Scriptures says, the man was found full of demons, crying out, and cutting himself with stones but when he saw Jesus afar off, he ran and worshipped him. (Mark 5:1-6) After Jesus commanded the unclean spirit to leave that once bound man, the citizen of the town saw him <u>sitting</u>, and <u>clothed</u>, and in his <u>right</u> mind, and they <u>were</u> afraid.

Imagine that! Glory unto to God! This man was at his last phase of life, inflicting pain upon himself but he still had the will to run to Jesus for peace. My brothers and sisters, we too have the same right as the man, who was possessed with a Legion of demons, and can run to the feet of Jesus and worship Him, because in His presence there is fullness of power, joy, peace, healing, restoration, and deliverance! He will set you on solid ground, and clothe you in righteousness, and renew your troubled mind with righteous thinking.

Jesus promises to never leave you nor push you away. It is His hearts' desire that all come into the knowledge of Him and surrender their life to Him. He is able to heal any manner of sickness and disease, physically and spiritually! He is the Way, Truth, and the Life! He is the Lord of all! He is the Savior of humanity! He is the Beginning and the End! Alpha and Omega! He is God!

People may not understand the change the Lord will do in your life, and may even fear you but don't stop yourself from being set free form the strongholds of spiritual wickedness, for the Son of God came to set the captive free and has all authority and power in His hand. Be free in the mighty name of Jesus Christ of Nazareth, the Son of the True and Living God of Abraham, Isaac, and Jacob!

13

Power of the Holy Ghost

<u>Acts 1:8</u>
But ye shall receive power, after that the Holy Ghost is come upon you; and ye shall be witnesses unto Me both in Jerusalem, and in all Judaea, and in Samaria, And unto the uttermost part of the earth.

Power is the special and peculiar prerogative of God, and God alone. "Twice have I heard this; that power belongs unto God." God is God; and power belongs to Him. If he delegates a portion of it to his creatures, yet still it is His power. The Father hath power; for by His word were the heavens made, and all the hosts of them; by his strength all things stand, and through Him they fulfill their destiny. The Son hath power; for, like His Father, He is the Creator of all things; "Without Him was not anything made that was made," and "by Him all things consist."

There are three ways to look at the uniqueness of the Holy Ghost. First, the outward and visible displays of it; second, the inward and spiritual manifestations of it; and third, the future and expected works thereof. The power of the Spirit will thus, I trust, be made clearly present to your souls. First, we can view the power of the Spirit in the OUTWARD AND VISIBLE DISPLAYS OF IT.

The power of the Sprit has not been dormant; it has exerted itself. The Spirit of God has done much already; more than could have been accomplished by any being except the Infinite, Eternal, and Almighty God, of whom the Holy Spirit is one person. There are four works which are the outward and manifest signs of the power of the Spirit; creation works; resurrection works; works of attestation, or of witness; and works of grace. Of each of these works I shall speak very briefly.

First, the Spirit has manifested the omnipotence of his power in creation works; for though not very frequently in Scripture, yet sometimes creation is ascribed to the Holy Ghost, as well as to the Father and the Son. The creation of the heavens above is said to be the work of God's Spirit. Psalms 104:29 reads; "Thou hidest thy face, they are troubled; thou takest away their breath, they die, and return to their dust. Thou sendest forth thy Spirit, they are created; and thou renewest the face of the earth." So that the creation of every man is the work of the Spirit; and the creation of all life, and all flesh-existence in this world, is as much to be ascribed to the power of the Spirit, as the first garnishing of the heavens, or the fashioning of the crooked serpent.

But if you look in the first chapter of Genesis, you will there see more particularly set forth that peculiar operation of power upon the universe which was put forth by the Holy Spirit; you will then discover what was his special work. The scriptures read in Genesis 1:2 that the earth was without form, and void; and darkness was upon the face of the deep. And the Spirit of God moved upon the face of the waters."

We know not how remote the period of the creation of this globe may be-certainly many millions of years before the time of Adam. It was entirely "without form and void; and darkness were upon the face of the deep." The Spirit came, and stretching his broad wings, bade the darkness disperse, and as he moved over it, all the different portions of matter came into their places, and it was no longer "without form, and void;" but became round, like its sister planets, and moved, singing the high praises of God-not discordantly, as it had done before, but as one great note in the vast scale of creation. This you see, then, is the power of the Spirit.

Though our Lord Jesus was born of a woman, and made in the likeness of sinful flesh, yet, the power that begat Him was entirely in God the Holy Spirit-as the Scriptures express it, "The Holy One of Israel shall overshadow thee." He was begotten, as the Apostles' Creed says, begotten of the Holy Ghost. "That holy thing which is born of thee shall be called the Son of the Highest."

A second manifestation of the Holy Spirit's power is to be found in the resurrection of the Lord Jesus Christ. If ye have ever studied this subject, ye have perhaps been rather perplexed to find that sometimes the resurrection of Jesus is ascribed to himself. By His own power and Godhead He could not be held by the bond of death, but as He willingly gave up his life He had power to take it up again.

In another portion of Scripture, you find it ascribed to God the Father: "He raised Him up from the dead:" "He hath God the Father exalted." It is said in Scripture that the Holy Spirit raised Jesus Christ. Now, all these things were true. He was raised by the Father Because the Father said, "Loose the prisoner-let him go. Justice is satisfied. My law requires no more satisfaction-vengeance has had its due-let him go."

Here He gave an official message, which delivered Jesus from the grave. He was raised by His own majesty and power, because He had a right to come out and therefore "burst the bonds of death could no longer hold Him." But the Spirit as to that energy which His mortal frame received, by which it rose again from the grave after having lain there for three days and nights, raised Him. If you want proofs of this you must open your Bible again, 1 Peter 3:18. "For Christ also hath once suffered for sins, the just for the unjust, that He might bring us to God, being put to death in the flesh but quickened by the Spirit."

The resurrection of Christ, then, was effected by the agency of the Spirit! And here we have a noble illustration of His omnipotence. Could you have stepped, as angels did, into the grave of Jesus, and seen his sleeping body, you would have found it cold as any other corpse. Lift up the hand; it falls by the side. Look at the eye; it is glazed. And there is a death-thrust, which must have annihilated life. See his hands: the blood distills not from them. They are cold and motionless. Can that body live? Can it start up? Yes, and be an illustration of the might of the Spirit. For when the power of the Spirit came on Him, as it was when it fell upon the dry bones of the valley, "He arose in the majesty of His divinity, bright and shining, astonished the watchmen so that they fled away; yea, He arose no more to die, but to live forever, King of kings and Prince of the kings of the earth."

The third of the works of the Holy Spirit, which have so wonderfully demonstrated His power, are works of witnessing. When Jesus went into the stream of baptism in the river Jordan, the Holy Spirit descended upon him like a dove, and proclaimed Him God's Beloved Son. And when afterwards Jesus Christ raised the dead, when He healed the leper, when He spoke to diseases and they fled apace, when demons rushed in thousands from those who were possessed of them, it was done by the power of the Spirit.

The Spirit dwelt in Jesus without measure, and by that power all those miracles were worked. The Holy Spirit has power omnipotent, even the power of God. Once more, if we want another outward and visible sign of the power of the Spirit, we may look at the works of grace.

Let the gospel be preached and the Spirit poured out, and you will see that it has such power to change the conscience, to ameliorate the conduct, to raise the debased, to chastise and to curb the wickedness of the race that you must glory in it. I say, there is nothing like the power of the Holy Ghost. Only let that come, and, indeed, everything can be accomplished. The Holy Ghost has power over men's hearts.

Now, men's hearts are very hard to affect. If you want to get at them for any worldly object, you can do it. The Spirit alone has power over man's heart. Do you ever try your power on a heart? If any man thinks that a minister can convert the soul, I wish he would try. He will soon find "it is neither by might nor power, but by My Spirit, saith the Lord."

There is one thing more stubborn than the heart: it is the will. The will can be a very stubborn thing; and in all men, if the will is once stirred up to opposition, there is nothing can be done with them. Once there was Free will in Paradise, a terrible mess Free will made there; for it spoiled all Paradise and turned Adam out of the garden. Free will was once in heaven; but it turned the glorious archangel out, and a third part of the stars of heaven fell into the abyss.

God desires to perfect us in holiness. There are two kinds of perfection, which we need: one is the perfection of justification in the person of Jesus; and the other is, the perfection of sanctification worked in him by the Holy Spirit. At present corruption still rests even in the breasts of the regenerate. At present the heart is partially impure.

At present there are still lusts and evil imaginations. But my soul rejoices to know that the day is coming when God shall finish the work which He has begun; and He shall present my soul, not only perfect in Christ, but perfect in the Spirit, without spot or blemish, or any such thing. And is it true that this poor depraved heart is to become as holy as that of God? And is it true that this poor spirit, which often cries, "O, wretched man that I am, who shall deliver me from the body of this sin and death!" shall get rid of sin and death? I shall have no evil things to vex my ears, and no unholy thoughts to disturb my peace. Oh happy hour! May it be hastened!

Another great work of the Holy Spirit, which is not accomplished, is the bringing on of the latter-day glory. In a few more years-I know not when, I know not how-the Holy Spirit will be poured out in a far different style from the present. There are diversities of operations; and during the last few years it has been the case that the diversified operations have consisted in very little pouring out of the Spirit.

Ministers have gone on in dull routine, continually preaching, preaching, preaching, and little good has been done. I do hope that perhaps a fresh era has dawned upon us, and that there is a better pouring out of the Spirit even now. For the hour is coming, and it may be even now is, when the Holy Ghost shall be poured out again in such a wonderful manner, that many shall run to and fro, and knowledge shall be increased-the knowledge of the Lord shall cover the earth as the waters cover the surface of the great deep; when his kingdom shall come, and his will shall be done on earth even as it is in heaven.

We are not going to be dragging on forever like Pharaoh, with the wheels off his chariot. My heart exults, and my eyes flash with the thought that very likely I shall live to see the outpouring of the Spirit; when "the sons and the daughters of God again shall prophesy, and the young men shall see visions and the old men shall dream dreams."

There shall be such a miraculous amount of holiness, such an extraordinary fervor of prayer, such a real communion with God, and so much vital faith, and such a spread of the doctrines of the cross, that every one will see that verily the Spirit is poured out like water, and the rains are descending from above. For that let us pray; let us continually labor for it, and seek it.

One more works of the Spirit, which will especially manifest His power-the general resurrection. We have reason to believe from Scripture, that the resurrection of the dead, it will be effected by the voice of God and of His Word (the Son), shall also be brought about by the Spirit. The same power that raised Jesus Christ from the dead shall also quicken your mortal bodies. The power of the resurrection is, perhaps, one of the finest proofs of the works of the Spirit.

My friends, if this earth could but have its mantle torn away for a little while, if the green sod could be cut from it, and we could look about six feet deep into its bowels, what a world it would seem! What should we see? We should see bones, carcasses, and rottenness, and worms and corruption. And you will wonder: Can these dry bones live? Can they start up? Yes!

"In a moment, in the twinkling of an eye, at the last trump, the dead shall be raised." He speaks; they are alive! See them scattered! Bone comes to his bone! See them naked; flesh comes upon them! See them still lifeless; "Come from the four winds, O breath, and breathe upon these slain!" When the wind of the Holy Spirit comes, they live; and they stand upon their feet an exceeding great army.

The Holy Spirit of God is very powerful, compassionate, understanding, and protective. The power of the Holy Ghost can change the heart and mind of any man you may be lead to witness to about the gospel of Jesus Christ. We must understand the power of the Spirit is our power; the power of the Spirit is our might. Once again my brothers and sisters if this is the power of the Spirit, why should you doubt anything? Do not doubt the Spirit's power. Go out and labor with this conviction, that the power of the Holy Ghost is able to do anything.

And now, lastly, to anyone who are living in ways contrary to the ways of God. What is there to be said to you about this power of the Spirit? There is hope for you. I cannot save you but I know my Master can. That is my consolation.

God has the power and desire to save you as well as anybody else. The Holy Ghost is able to break your heart and change your heart and justify you in God. He is able to bring anyone to Jesus and make you willing to receive forgiveness in the day of His power. The Baptism of the Holy Spirit is God's way of empowering us to manifest His love to His Church and to cleanse us and make us holy.

We need therefore to acknowledge that love is necessary for the proper use of the Gifts - faith works by love.(Galatians 5:6) Love edifies others (1Corinthians 8:1) as God has shown His love for you by giving you faith to believe in and trust in and cling to and rely on Jesus. You must be willing to turn away from of anything or anyone that would hold you back from experiencing and walking in His fullness through the Baptism in the Holy Spirit. Ask Him for it. Receive it. Freely it has been given to you - now freely give (Matthew 10:8)

The Holy Ghost has a variety of roles including witnessing of the Father and His Son, revealing the truth, cleansing sins, and giving us comfort and peace. One of the most important roles of the Holy Ghost is to witness of Heavenly Father and Jesus. This means that the Holy Ghost testifies to the truth of their existence. By the power of the Holy Ghost ye may know the truth of all things. The Holy Ghost sanctifies those who have turned away from their sinful deeds and remain sincere in their heart.

I also believe the Holy Ghost can also comfort and give us peace when we are in need, "But the Comforter, which is the Holy Ghost, whom the Father will send in my name, He shall teach you all things, and bring all things to your remembrance, whatsoever I have said unto you. Peace I leave with you, my peace I give unto you: not as the world gives, give I unto you. Let not your heart be troubled, neither let it be afraid" (John 14:26-27.)

A person may feel the Holy Ghost in many different ways, called the fruits of the spirit and the still small voice. The Holy Ghost enters our mind and heart, which anyone can hear, but one must receive the Gift of the Holy Ghost for it to linger with them always.

In the Bible Paul teaches that, "The fruit of the Spirit is love, joy, peace, longsuffering, gentleness, goodness, faith, meekness, temperance..." (Galatians 5:22-23.) We can also feel the Holy Ghost through thoughts, warnings, ideas, and comfort. The Lord can speak to us through the Holy Ghost as a "still small voice" just as he did with Elijah, "And, behold, the LORD passed by, and a great and strong wind rent the mountains, and brake in pieces the rocks before the LORD; but the LORD was not in the wind: and after the wind an earthquake; but the LORD was not in the earthquake: And after the earthquake a fire; but the LORD was not in the fire: and after the fire a still small voice" (1 Kings 19:11-12.)

To me the still small voice is when the Holy Ghost speaks to our spirit and because it's a spiritual sensation we have to "listen" more closely to recognize it. Often the whisperings from the Holy Ghost come into our mind and/or heart. I think this is how I most often feel or sense the guiding influence of the Spirit. "Yea, behold, I will tell you in your mind and in your heart, by the Holy Ghost, which shall come upon you and which shall dwell in your heart. It doesn't matter who you are, you can feel the guidance of the Holy Ghost. You have probably felt his power without realizing it because our Heavenly Father uses the Holy Ghost to guide us, inspire us, and help us make right choices.

Throughout my life I have felt the influence of the Holy Ghost in many different ways. Feeling the Holy Ghost is different than feeling our own emotions, like watching a sad movie that makes you cry although sometimes feeling the Holy Ghost does make me cry. I often feel peace and joy when touched by the influence of the Holy Ghost and often it just comes as a thought of something I must do, something I hadn't been thinking of. At times I have also felt a warm, tingly sensation come over me and I know that my Heavenly Father loves me. He speaks softly to my heart and reminds me quit often, "Myron I Love you!"

The Gift of the Holy Ghost is received right after baptism, by the laying on of hands, and can be with us always if we keep the commandments. Through the baptism by fire, which comes from the Gift of the Holy Ghost, we can continue to be cleansed from our sins.

I received the Gift of the Holy Ghost is given by the laying on of hands from my pastor at the age of 17 and felt an electronic shock feel my body yet at the same time I felt peace fill my heart and my view literally changed at that moment.

When the Lord prompts my heart to minister or I hear His chosen speak His Word, I feel heat consume my insides and I often time found myself bursting out in tongues of praise unto the Father God.

I can tell you receiving the gift of the Holy Ghost is very dangerous and is true in context with Acts 2. This "fire" from the gift of the Holy Ghost cleanses us from our sins when we repent and is what purifies and sanctifies us. Now the Lord refers to sin and blasphemy against the Holy Spirit as unforgivable sin. (Blasphemy against the Holy Spirit is also referenced in Matthew 12:31-32 and Luke 12:10). According to Merriam - Webster dictionary the word "blasphemy" means "the act of insulting or showing contempt or lack of reverence for God; the act of claiming the attributes of deity; irreverence toward something considered sacred."

The Bible says in 1 John 1:9, "If we confess our sins, He is faithful and just and will forgive us our sins and purify us from all unrighteousness." (NIV) This verse, and many others that speak of God's forgiveness, seem to be in contrast with Mark 3:29 and this concept of an unforgivable sin. So what constitutes blasphemy against the Holy Spirit, the eternal sin that can never be forgiven? So in conclusion, of this chapter I would like to encourage all who have come into the knowledge of Jesus Christ and the power of the God walk in the authority given to you by Jesus.

Again, I encourage you to come into the knowledge of Jesus, believe He is Lord and He died for our sins on Calvary cross but God raised Him up from the grave and He now is sitting in the right hand of the Father, calling you to be His friend for Jesus cares for you more than His life, for He gave His life that you and I may live.

Answer the call of forgiveness of sins and love, my dear brother and sister. Confess with your mouth and believe in your heart and you shall be saved from the punishment of sin. Jesus offers salvation of your souls from hell freely and without His salvation and eternal love no man can enter into paradise. He promises to never leave you nor forsake you by sending His Spirit into your heart to guide, protect, and equip you with power over any and all temptations that leads to sin.

14

My Brother, My Friend

Proverbs 18:24
A man that hath friends must show himself friendly:
and there is a friend that sticketh closer than a brother.

In this journey of life, I have come to a crossroad of whether to uphold to Christianity or the true ways of God. Christianity within itself is both dangerous and deadly and I believe there are several of children being forced to accept Christianity or whatever religious belief in the home instead of truly understanding the God of creation and who they are in perspective of life.

As stated before, my father and mother forced us to go to church and accept the teaching of the proposed leader of the organization. There was a great lack of communication in the home therefore our relationship with one another were second-hand. I was personally taught to utilize my gifts and talents for church and to sing outside of the church would be hypocritical. Therefore growing up I shied away from performances in clubs, schools, and talent shows. As I reached mid teens, several of my friends ventured off in the music business and earn music recording deals and I then began to wonder; "There has to be more to life than just singing in the church!"

I began to compose music at the age of 13 and my brother would always inspire me to go further in my music endeavor but again religion killed that dream. Deep inside my heart yearned to excel beyond the four walls of church, but lacked the know-how. I clapped and danced to the music of the band but felt empty inside because I knew that God had placed a unique gift of singing and healing to share with the world, but according to the church rules, I had to be with a ministry organization or simply wait until I were recognized than my turn was up.

There are so many people, both young and seasoned of age, lost behind religion; poisoned to go to church, church, and more church but do not know who they are! There is so much power and control in religion that men have been at war since the beginning of creation. Now the war that I fought was against self in hopes of finding my identity. The first step in finding my identity was to deny self and not judge others. Through the scope of Christianity I felt as a king but never knew God, because I lacked the love of God for others.

In the process of growing and adapting to life in general, I found myself in a lot of trouble with people and the law. As a sense of comfort, at the age of fourteen, I was initiated into the Crip gang and stabbed a young man in the neck in junior high school and was charged with assault with deadly weapon. I didn't find myself in a lot of fights but I did have a lot of confrontations with my peers, and opposite gangs. Besides all the trouble I got in, I always found a job to work at and hustled "secretly" with my friends. I began selling and smoking weed on a daily basis knowing that such lifestyle is not what I was destined to be participating in. God sealed me for His divine purpose and I knew it.

The process of surrendering to God and accepting change in my life was painful. Most of the things I got involved in were to ease the pain of loneliness in my heart. While attending high school, I would go to the clubs and hang with the crowd but always felt as though I were the only one there. My attendance and performance at school was horrible and I found myself in the face of police and my mom always told me to "stay away from the crowd" but I had a hard heart and thought I knew everything. I can clearly remember when I working at Avis rental car, in the year 2000, and my mother told me not to take the cars home, but I refused to listen.

My life took a great turn for destruction, when I had taken a car to the rental drop off place and exchanged for another one. Instead of going back to work, I called my cousin and told him I had a rental car so he asked me to come and hang with him. So I did. When arriving home, my mother said she had a feeling that something bad was about to happen to me and I should return the car back that night but I didn't. My brothers and sisters, scriptures are true: Pride leads to destruction and a haughty spirit before a fall. Now what a great fall I had!

Now the rental car lot was closed on the weekend so I thought I was not monitored but God knew and the tracking system on the cars were still active. Now that I look back at my foolish actions, it's funny how I was arrested. The moment I walked out the house, there were more than 5 police cars and two undercover cars surrounding the whole apartments we lived in. More than 6 cops came to me at gunpoint while the undercover cop placed the handcuffs on me. I almost vomited the moment I saw them because judgment had been set against me for my actions.

I plead guilty to auto theft and received 4 years probation. Truthfully my life was in shambles. I held on to guilt, anger, and bitterness and literally was ready to explode at any moment. Due to shame, I left my parents home and stayed with my friend. I maintained working and paid my probation fees for 2 years. In the meantime, I met my dear friend and brother, Thomas Earl Gaines, about 10 years ago at a community college where he worked.

We must understand God will use any situation or person to steer us in the right path. I believe God had divinely set me in the path of righteousness through Thomas Earl Gaines, from that moment on. Again I held onto guilt, anger, and bitterness, and had so much hatred in my heart towards my parents and others around me. I even blamed them for my foolish ways, but deep inside I knew and know that my parents lead us in the ways of God.

The moment I met Thomas he looked at me, smiled and said "My brother, Jesus!" It was very strange to me at that moment because he didn't ask for my name or if I knew the Lord, he simply looked me in the eyes firmly and said "My brother, Jesus!" Those words are the most powerful words I have ever heard someone say to me. Quite often my heart burns within hearing his voice saying those words repeatedly. There is something about the name of Jesus, and I could literally see the presence of God on my dear friend.

Thomas Earl Gaines was an ordinary man with a heart that exemplified the characteristics of Almighty God. He once told me that life is nothing if you do not have a relationship with God through His Son Jesus. He was truly rich in spirit and full of the love of God. He lacked nothing spiritually or physically from my view of seeing him. He loved life and every nationality that we can think of.

I remember times when we would sit and have bible study in college and people from different nationalities would come and sit down and ask what we were doing and he'd simply say "Jesus!" From such bold declaration, I watched many walk away cursing, and also many immediately sit down and gain knowledge of who Jesus is and accept Him into their life as Lord and Savior. He lived by this slogan: "It's not about me, it's all about Jesus!" Little did he know, or maybe he knew, I broke away from the religious and traditions of men and developed a true relationship with God due to his actions.

Thomas humbly showed me the love of God in front of everyone and the love of God for others began to fill my heart. Man, I love my brother because when I was hungry, he gracefully feed me. When I needed someone to talk to, he always made his schedule available to talk. He NEVER pointed out my faults or looked at me as a stranger. Thomas is truly a son of God and an angel. There were several nights we would just hang out and study the Word of God and the presence of God would literally filled the environment. There were several nights we would bass in the presence of God and see clouds of glory in the atmosphere and stand in awe! Truly the power and majesty of God is real and still active, my friend!

There were moments we would just say "Jesus" and the power of God would hit us, causing us to speak in the utterance of unknown tongues, crying out to the majesty of the Lord. I can't truly remember being able to just lay my head on my fathers' shoulder and cry but I was able to cry on Thomas shoulder and feel the warmth of a true father. I believe every son need to have the warmth of his father. I hope you all understand and appreciate those who have been an impact on your life. Thomas taught me Jesus not the religious views and aspects of Christianity. We would dissect the Word of God for hours and just bass in the presence of God after worth.

I will never forget the moment I had found myself in more trouble at the college; chasing the ladies or stealing computers and the campus police banned me from going there. While suspended, Thomas took the time to speak with the President of the college, requesting my return to school, and she allowed me to continue attending school there.

There was so much favor being manifest on me behalf and I thank the Lord God for it. He and I would get in the talent shows at the college and instead of entertaining the crowd, God lead us to worship in the midst of the program and over 10 people received Jesus into their life and the program was turned upside down for the glory of God.

There were several moments I would not have money for rent or simply lunch and God would place on his heart to bless me over abundantly without my notice. He would strategically call me and ask me what I were doing and say he would meet me wherever I were at. He would reach out and give me a hand shake or "dap" and slip the money in my hand and simply began to pray in agreement for blessing on my life and the finances received.

My brothers and sisters, I tell you the truth, Thomas never gave me less than $20 dollars, on more than 15 occasions within the 10 years of knowing him. The Lord is truly great, compassionate, and understanding. I dare not boast in self, or what God blessed Thomas to do for me, but rather the goodness of God. When Thomas was blessed with clothing, money, or anything materialistically, he would call me up and bless me in all aspects. I lacked nothing nor do I lack anything because of the unfailing love of God.

Thomas Earl Gaines understood the principle of "giving" because he literally gave his life for me, by never considering himself more than anyone. His walk, talk, and lifestyle was similar to the life of Jesus and many who have come to know Thomas would vow to say the same. No he was not perfect but he did strive to walk in the perfect (complete) image of Christ.

Thomas taught me that that being a man is not about how much money one has or their status in life, but rather ones' conduct in life and respect for others. Again in the process of learning more about God on the perspective of a relationship not religion, I learned the truths that Jesus and God are one-not separable as some church leaders teach.

I would like to leave you with this: Jesus tells a parable about what it means to love your neighbor. There was a man traveling from Jerusalem to Jericho. On his journey he was attacked by thieves, robbed, and left for dead. A priest and a Levite both passed by him A Samaritan helped him, showing he loves his neighbor. We should do the same.

I was once that man traveling from the highest point in my life and ended up in the lowest point of my life, stripped away from joy, happiness, and left for dead but God rescued me and truly revealed Himself through Thomas Earl Gaines. The walls of religion are now broken! I am a changed man forever! Glory to God!! To all his family, rest assure Myron DeShun Banks love you all from the least to the greatest and have come into to the knowledge of Jesus Christ through your son, brother, or uncle Mr. Thomas Earl Gaines!

He was my father, brother, best friend, and willing yet humbly taught me "Jesus" not Christianity by his actions! I will forever love and respect him although he is not presently with us. No doubt he is resting peacefully in the presence of the Lord God Almighty, ready to see our Lord and Savior Jesus Christ! My heart is free! I humbly yet boldly dedicate this book to him and his precious family, but ultimately my Lord and Savior Jesus of Nazareth.

15

Wrestling with our First Love

Revelations 2:2-4

I know your works, labor, patience, and how you cannot stand those who are evil, and you have tried those who say they are apostles and are not, and have found them to be liars. You have persevered and have patience, and have labored for my namesake, and have not become weary. Nevertheless, I have this against you; that you have left your First Love!

God longs for each of His children to express true love to Him. In the midst of all our doing, God is willing and able to speak to us, if we have a desire to listen to His precious voice. His voice often comes in the middle of the night or at early hours of morning (3am-5am), when our hearts are most unedited and vulnerable. At first, we may mistake the source of His voice and assume it is just our imagination. We toss and turn in our bed, and He whispers again: Aren't you thirsty? Listen to your heart... There is something missing!"

Religion doesn't allow you to freely worship God nor will you truly love others. Without a true relationship with God, Satan's chains bind us tight around the post of religion, which ultimately leads to sin against God. But a true and honest relationship with God breaks the chains of tradition and religion: alongside doubt, heartache, pain, poverty, and condemnation. We deserve only the wrath of a holy Righteous God, but instead, He reaches down towards us with His ultimate expression of love. We should not hesitate to show our true love to God through obedience and humility.

We sometimes find it hard and far more difficult to adore the Messiah who saved our souls from death, through church acts of worship; where we are timed and expected to keep our composure, until we grasp the fullness of who Christ is. Christ is spirit, so no matter how much we jump around and quote text from his word; if our hearts aren't truly in relations with Him, all is void.

Worship involves a life-long process of learning to simply "let go". Sadly many believers are so fascinated with their appearance, what people say or think towards them, that they miss the presence of God. When they worship, it is only their personal emotions. We have a deep inner craving in us that He alone can fill. He created us to love Him! We are created to worship Him and Him alone!

Man alone sulks in his cave, with all the technology and wonderful knowledge, we cannot compare to God. Only as we acknowledge the emptiness that cries for worship, can the constant unrest within us be settled. Our search for God will be most meaningful when we realize the utter bareness of a soul separated for Him.

In various degrees many of us are guilty of seeking satisfaction through intellectual, emotional, or physical stimulation. There once was in a man a true happiness of what remains to him only the mark and empty trace, which he, in vain, tries to fill from all his surroundings. Seeking from things absent the help he does not obtain in thing present. But these are all inadequate because an infinite and immutable object. Only God Himself can fill the infinite abyss.

The life of the heart is a great place of mystery, yet we have many expressions to help us express this flame of the human soul. In the end, it doesn't matter how well we have performed, or what we have accomplished- a life without heart, is meaningless. For out of this wellspring of our souls flow all meaningful work, all real worship, and sacrifice.

There is a secret place set within each of our hearts. It often goes unnoticed, we can barely put words to it, but yet it guides us throughout the days of our lives. You may not always be aware of your search, and there are times you have abandoned looking altogether, but again and again, it returns to us; this yearning that cries out for the life we all desire. Seasons may pass before we grasp what lies deep within us, which is peace, because life comes to all as a mystery, and only one person is able to reveal the mystery of life: Jesus the Savior of Humanity.

Our days are confusing and we hold to assumed birthdays, traditions, and holidays. The greatest failure for mankind is to give up in life and destroy his life. Nothing is of great importance than the life of our deep heart. Once we find the answer, we can than walk in peace and the power of God towards mankind.

Life has taught us to prove we are someone by our career, relationship, or success, but God looks beyond the scope of life, and sees in our hearts the truth of who we are. We have been programmed in the church to work rather than to have a true relationship with God.

Communion with God has been replaced with activity for God. The true story of every person in this world is no the story you see. The true story of each person is the journey of his or her heart. In a broad sense worship is inseparable and an expression of life. We were made to worship just as we were made to breathe. There is an inward craving to worship; even the most decided believer could be swayed away with the pleasures of life.

A Mature Relationship with the Lord embodies three components: KNOWLEDGE, COVENANT, and WORSHIP. So I ask you who are you intimate with? God or man? When I began to look at the church cults and its rituals, I asked the Lord to show me what He wanted from all who love Him. He clearly spoke to me and said; "INTIMACY." To be intimate with someone means to have closeness, likeness, or same desires. There were several of times I would literally do all I could to please the leaders of the church, wearing myself down by being in all sorts of organizations, like many still bound to that chain; seeking for recognition or promotion to a greater position.

While asleep; God revealed myself; filthy and bound in chains, being tormented by demons. I cried out still unable to understand the vision. God then spoke to me and asked me, "Myron, who are you being intimate with, Me or man?" Ashamed and convicted because He rebuked me of my self-righteous deeds: I cried out with repentance to God and He forgave me! In the passage Matthew 7:21-23, I believe Jesus is warning Spirit-filled believers who have seen the power of God flowing in their ministries and life. Truthfully He is saying: "Even all that is not enough, I want your heart. You need to put away sin, independence and let Me direct you."

If we have been sinning willfully, or we have not been doing what God wants us to do, the answer is to repent, and renew our love for God. God is willing to forgive - we must be willing to be changed and go in a different way. Jesus will say to these people, "I never knew you." They did all these great things, but He did not have a close relationship with them.

The word know, "**ginosko**" in the Greek, refers in this context to an intimate relationship of union and approval. That is the kind of relationship a believer needs to have with Christ. Jesus will not say those words of condemnation in Matthew 7:21-23 to someone who truly loves Him and obeys His commandments. God approves and truly works together with those who love Him. If we love the Lord, we will be looking to

Him for power to overcome sin before we look for miraculous displays of the power of signs and wonders.

Not all are willing to embrace it, due to the fear and misapprehension generated by false teachings. However, the most important thing we must have is true love for God. A faith in God that has no love for God in it is not saving faith. Because of who Christ is, and what He has done for us, we should all be moved to seek after Him and consistently please Him out of gratitude and holy fear.

There is an emphasis in the church today, which equates any idea of the fear of God with legalism. But someone truly in love with our awesome God will appreciate Him, and if they do sin, will be quick to confess and repent before God. A faith in God that has no love for God in it is not saving faith. Because of who Christ is, and what He has done for us, we should all be moved to seek after Him and consistently please Him out of gratitude and holy fear.

16

Power and Control in Religion

Matthew 23:1-7
Then spake Jesus to the multitude, and to his disciples, saying
The scribes and the Pharisees sit in Moses' seat: All therefore whatsoever they bid you observe, that observe and do; but do not ye after their works: for they say, and do not. For they bind heavy burdens and grievous to be borne, and lay them on men's shoulders. But they themselves will not move them with one of their fingers. But all their works they do for to be seen of men: they make broad their phylacteries, and enlarge the borders of their garments, and love the uppermost rooms at feasts, and the chief seats in the synagogues, and greetings in the markets, and to be called of men, Rabbi, Rabbi.

Religion was created to supposedly help us worship God, but religion sometimes takes control. I believe most religions start with the object of focusing on God, and worshiping him. Somewhere along the way the religious leaders and the congregation loose focus of God, and start to focus on what they believe should and should not be done. This is not a recent problem either.

Even Jesus had this problem with the religious leaders of his day. One of the major problems Jesus saw was the leaders took over the worship of God, and created it into what they wanted it to be. Weather this was done to have control over the people, or that they themselves actually got so lost in what they *perceived* as the law that they lost sight of what they were suppose to be doing.

There were many more man made laws they created, than what God actually revealed to them. These laws became so many, that most people lost sight as to what God really wanted. By that time, they may not have really cared when Jesus stood up to them. Yes, we still have this same problem in today's society as well where man's religious laws over rides God's laws. We loose focus of God and what He wants. We loose focus of why we are worshiping God. There are some religious leaders who use God and Jesus to control the congregation, and to increase their wealth.

At the same time, there are those leaders who have a heart for God, and what God wants. They are leading their people in the right direction, and practicing and doing what Jesus taught. Now the question becomes how to discern the ones who are following after God's heart, and those who are out for themselves. The best way I know how to do this is to read your Bible. Get to know God's words well. Don't be afraid to question what your pastor is saying. Please, don't stand up in the middle of service, and confront Him then and there.

The best way I believe to do this is to make notes in church. When you are at home, look up all the scriptures he mentioned. Do a study of what the pastor is saying. What I look for in this search is there other scripture to back up what was being spoken about. I believe the Bible will always back it self up. Where the ideas come from in the first place? Did it come from a strong teaching in the Bible? Several quotes scattered throughout the Bible, or from only one or two verses? Is it a repeating theme throughout the Bible?

I am very weary when someone claims the Bible says something, but really cannot back it up. I'm also weary when someone says you have to be a scholar/theologian to really know what the Bible says. I believe God created the Bible so everyone could read and understand His word. I do believe He can have multiple meanings in a verse. I do not believe that those meanings will be so well hidden that it would actually change the basic meaning of the verse when it is read.

This is also where we get many conflicts as to what the Bible actually says such as once saved always saved verses you can backslide and fall out of grace and salvation. This is where you really need to do your own research on what the Bible says with an open mind. Don't make the Bible say what you want it to say, but see what it is actually telling you. Once you know what the Bible says on that subject, and have it in your heart, no one can deceive you.

Sometimes it is hard to tell which religion or religious leader is following God. The best way to get out from under the control of religion is to know God's words. If the religion or leader of your church practices God's words, does not have you practicing things the Bible tells you not to do, and does not have you doing things that are not even talked about in the Bible to get saved, repent, and living the life Jesus wants you to, then you know you are in the right place. If you find out that the church you are in does have you practicing things that are against God's word, then leave that church and/or religion, and find somewhere that does practice and preach God's word.

17

Step Out of Religion

Into a Relationship with God

Mark 7:6-8
He answered and said unto them, well hath Esaias prophesied of you hypocrites, as it is written; this people honored Me with their lips, but their heart is far from Me.

I have come to realization that for nearly 10 years I was walking in a path that was leading me to hell, although I professed I was a Christian. I professed "Christianity" and even talked the talk: *"God bless you my brother, God bless you my sister, etc!"* When I would go to church, I had the church walk, talk, and even the clothing attire that would *"make-up"* a *"Christian."*

I shouted and danced to the music and even sang demons out of people but...my heart was truly filthy and I was fake. When I left church I would go to the club, run the streets and abuse women both physically and sexually. Church was simply a building I went to, to make my parents or the crowd happy yet I always left wondering... *"Man there has to be more to this church thing than just going. Why do I feel empty inside?"* God clearly spoke to me in a soft voice, *"Myron, your ways and your heart is not right before me!" You must be willing to change your lifestyle! The process will be painful and the seeds you have sown throughout your life you must reap, but you will not die!"*

I was taught through the views of many pastors and leaders of an organization that when one confesses Jesus as the Messiah and way to Heaven, he or she is forgiven of all their sins and becomes a Christian. Oh was I wrong and are they wrong. There must be an evident change of our lifestyle that exemplifies the characteristics of Jesus the Son of God. Of course, we are not complete in the ways of righteousness but we must strive earnestly on a daily basis to live righteous and free ourselves from sinful ways of living.

Sadly, I come to realization also, that many have been taught about religion instead of having a relationship with God. For quite a while I held on to a religious view of life. I boldly challenged people in their faith contrary to mine and felt I were the voice of God or His right-hand man. Due to such religious ways, love was choked out of me and my mind was bound to hate those who didn't believe that Jesus is the Messiah of the world.

I foolishly separated myself from them and thought that I was walking the *good walk of faith*. I openly refused to love them because of their beliefs contrary to mine and became angry toward unbelievers, condemning and judging them as though I were God. The church had become my throne, and all who were not believers were my prisoners. I read out their sins and gave them their sentencing. I held the **law-book** firmly in my hand, read it to others, but never read the law-book for myself! I fell into sin daily but seldom turned away from them and asked for Gods forgiveness.

Again the Lord spoke to me and said; *"Myron when you offend my people you offend Me and My wrath will come upon you! You are not my disciple, just look at how you are treating your fellow brothers and sisters!"* I tell you the truth; Myron DeShun Banks was doomed for eternal punishment in hell fire for having hatred in his heart toward others. I held up the banner of "Christianity" but my lifestyle was not in relationship to Christ.

I assumed that anyone from a Middle Eastern country was evil and their beliefs were false. I openly prejudged them and kept away from them. It was not until I did intense studying on the many religions of the world and realized that many of their beliefs are similar. The only exclusive thing I noticed is the different gods and goddesses, and ways of worship in the religions. I've learned to embrace others no matter their religious beliefs and just love and treat them as I desire to be treated believing that God will change our hearts, because when I see a person I don't see their religion but rather I see a person. Only in time will a person share their beliefs and views of life upon our receptiveness to them.

If we want to truly establish a relationship with God we must first deny our own way of thinking (deny self) and love our neighbor as ourselves and not prejudge them or think of ourselves higher than others. We must be willing to spend time in prayer and meditation unto God on a daily basis.

We must be diligent in searching for truth in the ways of God and be bold yet humble enough to ask God questions pertaining to Himself and the desires He has for our life. I tell you the truth; the Lord will answer you when you call on Him with confidence and expectancy. He is our Father and He promises to answer us when we call on Him. I personally found out that Jesus is the way, the truth and the life, and He is the Lord of all lords and Kings of all kings. Therefore I make a daily effort to come into intimate knowledge of Him on a daily basis.

    I tell you the truth my brothers and sisters, to truly know the Lord Jesus and change your lifestyle will not be easy but I guarantee, you will reap good results if you faint not through the process. I challenge you to sit back and just think about your life and the many people who are currently connected to you. Get a sheet of paper and write out their names one by one. For each person write out the Pros and Cons (Good and Bad) for each one according to your personal view not theirs. This is just one process that is painful because many of our so called friends are not truly our friends if their results reveal more bad than good.

    Ask yourself after worth, will this person or that person lead me to a path that is destructive or to a path that is beneficial? I tell you the truth, the results (payment) we will receive for sin is Death but the results (payment) for righteousness is Life. I lost many friends because I chose to walk alone and trust God through the process of walking in the path that leads to eternal life. I tell you also, if you chose to walk in the path of righteousness many of your friends will not like it and will even criticize you but I encourage you not to worry about their slanderous words. Just know a better life is ahead for you through the Messiah Jesus Christ.

    Jesus spoke of a parable and said that He is the Vine and God is the Husbandman, any branch that does not produce fruits of righteousness God will pluck away and have cast into the fire. *(John 15)* He also said that a good tree can not bear bad fruit nor can a bad tree bear good fruit. Therefore, I ask myself quite often; *"Myron, are you doing things and living a lifestyle pleasing unto God before men?"*

    I have even gone to the extent of asking for accountability partners in my life who are not afraid to steer me in the right path when I get off course. Truthfully, there are times I do things that are not pleasing unto God yet I will not wander in such ways. We must be willing to change our lifestyle and with the strength of God, we will learn how to let God change our life, but only as we confess we are in need of His saving grace and power over sin.

I've learned through my personal walk with God, that when someone receives the power of God in their life, it not a dance that one does in church that proves they have changed, but rather ones' lifestyle outside of the church building. With the power of God, we can overcome sin, the same way Jesus did and live a life pleasing in the sight of both God and man. When we establish a relationship with God through His Son Jesus Christ we come in right-standing with God and co-heir of His heavenly kingdom.

Through the scope of *"Christianity"* I was taught I needed to dress a certain way to come to church, but when I established a relationship with Jesus I realized that no matter how one puts up an "image" if our heart is not right, none of it matters. Jesus will cleanse your heart and change you from the inside out.

I've also realized that no matter how far in the path of destruction I'd walked, the Lord was always there calling me to Himself. He is willing and able to save you and wash away all your sins. God desires that none perish but that all will come into the knowledge of Him and establish a relationship with Him. He promises to never leave you nor forsake you. He will be there available to all who call on Him with a sincere heart.

I was foolishly taught that coming to church and being part of the organizations were ways of showing others I loved God but God simply showed me differently. I didn't keep His commandments and refused to learn from the discipline I received for my disobedience and change. In order to receive the fullness of Gods anointing, blessing and promises, we have to do more then just fill the pews. I was also taught in somes churches that God, Jesus, and the Holy Ghost are three different people. But God revealed to me that He is One, just three different manifestations of Himself. As each one of us, we all are spirit, enclothed with flesh (body) and our soul is our thought, will, and emotion.

As I continue to gain intimate knowledge of God, I've discovered He is not concerned with the religious word "Christian." It's about your relationship with Him, not your religion. It's trusting in Jesus and what He did on the cross for you and me, not on what we can do for ourselves. It's not about ornate buildings, flamboyant preachers, or traditional rules.

Do you truly believe God is in heaven saying; *"oh there are my Christians followers, hey look at those Mormons and Jehovah Witnesses?! Hey those groups of people look like Muslims, Hindus, and Scientologist!* NO!! Or do you believe that He will say on Judgment Day; *"Hey I want all the Christians, Jews, and Muslims on my right side and all the Hindus, Scientologist, Buddhist on my left side!"* NO! He will simply separate the sheep from the goat.

Again, when we all stand before God on Judgment Day to give account for our deeds, I believe as stated in *Matthew 25:31-46*, He will separate the sheep from the goat and reward us according to our works. The sheep will be on His right side and the goats will be on his left side. Jesus took this opportunity to remind everyone that His church is not about religion--even casting out demons and performing miracles (see Matt 7)--but about loving our neighbors, especially the least of them, in a tangible way. Not just praying for them, or voting in their best interests. But rather getting out there and loving them personally. So much of what we do is just religious. We all should take heed and not think of ourselves as being secure because of our religion.

Many of us attend church regularly but no change takes place in our life. In many cases, it's because we hold to traditions and not a true relationship with God. If we truly love God we would love our neighbor, whether black, white, purple, blue, yellow or red and do whatever it takes to make sure that their needs are met. The Lord said that many people draw near to Him with their words, but their hearts are far from Him (Matthew 15:8). Our actual walk will be discovered by the way we act, not by the way we talk."

Intimate Worship is the key to Gods heart, and only way we can become more like Jesus. I can remember when I was about 23, I asked God to reveal some mysteries of His word and He told me to write out the word INTIMACY. So I wrote out INTIMACY. Then the Lord told me to say the word very slow, so I said it (in short) IN-TI-MA-CY. Then I began to hear the Lord say; *"Myron, Enter Me And See!"*

When you come into a relationship with someone, you gain intimate knowledge of that person and nothing or no one can deter you away from her or him. Well likewise it should be in our relationship with God. When we come into a relationship with God we should not allow anything or anyone deter us away from Him or what we know of Him. Jesus spent most of His time in prayer unto God, even if His disciples didn't understand.

We must be the same way. Just like it is important to exercise our physical body to stay fit and in good condition, it is important to exercise our spiritual body, through studying Gods word and through intimate prayer, that we may overcome the daily temptations and stress of life.

Someone had once said that seven days without prayer makes one weak. Prayer is the way that we, His branches, draw the nutrients we need from God the Vine to produce the fruit of His spirit in our lives. Ministry to God must come before ministry to people. God not only wants to speak to you, He also wants to show you deeper dimensions of Himself. If you do not love your enemies, you are walking in sin. If you do not love others despite their differences of beliefs, you are walking in sin. If you only fellowship with your brothers and sisters (spiritual), you are walking in sin. If you do not forgive those who have hurt you, you are walking in sin. We are all one kindred, (humans) but have different belief of living, and all have ways displeasing to the Lord. We need to stop belittling one another and walk in LOVE.

Starting with a love for God, one will tithe properly, also desire justice in this world, demonstrate mercy towards others and have faithfulness towards God. Starting from love, we can get the proper behavior that Jesus expected out of the Pharisees, and by extension, us. Jesus said, "I am the way and the truth and the life. No one comes to the Father except through Me." (John 14:6) You can't get to heaven by following rules laid down by other humans; you've got to have that relationship with God through faith in Jesus.

You do NOT have to have a license to preach the gospel, it is IN you. You do NOT have to obtain an evangelist position in the church to evangelize; Jesus has COMMANDED you. You do NOT have to know the bible from Genesis to Revelation or Revelation to Genesis, Jesus IS THE WORD MADE FLESH. You must rely on the guidance of the Holy Spirit which is the spirit of Jesus which lives in you and open your ears to His continual speaking and do as He commands without hesitation as though your life depends on Him, (which does) and so do the lost.

Now is the time to seek the Lord with your whole heart. Now is the time to allow Jesus Christ to wash you daily, over and over with His pure blood and cleanse your heart, of all unrighteousness. Now is the time to allow Him to be your Master, Guide, and God. Now is the time to obey His commandments and *"deny self."*

Now is the time to chase after God more than you do a job, career, success or money. Now is the time for us to walk in love and denounce our religious beliefs and establish relationship with God and walk in the fruit of the Spirit to others which is love, joy, peace, longsuffering, gentleness, goodness, faith, meekness, and temperance. (Galatians 5:19-26)

All the laws, moral codes, and commandments of God, are summed up in this: Love God and love your neighbor. And how do we love God? We love our neighbor (Matt 22:38-40) Love is the **fulfillment** of the law and draws man to the only true and wise God, not separation or rejection of them.

In closing, I would like to extend an invitation of salvation to all readers. For all who has not received the love of God, Jesus is standing at the door of your heart knocking so please answer the door. He will save your life from hells punishment and forgive you of all your sins. He promises to give you the love, peace, protection, and strength you need to survive in this deadly and poisonous world.

For anyone addicted to witch craft, pornography, masturbation, drugs, bisexuality or homosexuality, please turn away from those sinful ways, repent of them, ask Jesus to come into your heart and cleanse you of all sins, and be your Lord and God today. Receive the power of the Holy Ghost that you may overcome those wicked desires.

For all incarcerated behind physical bars, I want to let you know that I love you and Jesus Christ, the Messiah of the world loves you and will give you peace in the middle of your storm. Call on His precious name and He will be there for you, even in the midnight hour.

I would like to leave you with this: A man once fell on his knees before Christ and begged, "If you are willing, you can make me clean." Christ, "filled with compassion" replied, "I am willing; be clean" (Mark 1:40-41). We too can fall on our knees and acknowledge God's only provision for our sins. We too can hear, "I am willing; be clean." Christ willingly took God's righteous indignation upon Himself so that you don't have to; whoever accepts His death upon the cross as payment for their sins will be reconciled to the God whom they've offended. "All this is from God, who reconciled us to himself through Christ... God was reconciling the world to Himself in Christ, not counting men's sins against them... God made Him who had no sin to be sin for us, so that in Him we might become the righteousness of God" (2 Corinthians 5:18-21).

I pray that we all come in unison of the truth that Love is the answer and by no other way can we see God. God is not smiling down on His people and our sins have reached the heavens, before the return of the Messiah, the true church must be without spot, wrinkle, or blemish.

But as I speak; America cries, our churches will continue to divide, and our flag of honor will stay drenched in blood because of religion and traditions we hold to. We should be compelled in our heart to share the love that the God of this universe has given us and not focus on the material things of this world.

My dear brother and sister Judgment is soon to come and who can escape such judgment? Only those who have been sealed with the blood covenant of Jesus Christ the Son of the Living God! Will you accept God's love today while your blood still runs warm in your body? Jesus is standing there calling you with His arms open wide, ready to clear your troubled mind. Jesus loves you no matter who you are or the wrong you have ever done. Jesus Christ is the only way to heaven, so please believe in His works, redemptive blood, and His unfailing love. The days you hear the Lord's voice harden not your heart. He is calling you right now. Now is the time! NOW is the time! Tomorrow may be too late! STEP OUT OF RELIGION INTO TO RELATIONSHIP WITH GOD!!

www.ingramcontent.com/pod-product-compliance
Lightning Source LLC
Chambersburg PA
CBHW020012050426
42450CB00005B/436